CROWN

PLAYING IN THE SHADOWS

TOM RAVLIC

'A forensic examination of an industry that aims to hide in the shadows.'

Peter van Onselen, political editor, Network Ten

'It's a great effort making good use of all the official investigations. It's without moral panic about the Aussie addiction to gambling but exposes corporate, gangster and terrorist money laundering tricks, malfeasance, negligence but, most significantly, the total failure of regulatory controls. Tom Ravlic has done us all a great service in exposing the Crown and uncontrolled casino scandals.'

Quentin Dempster, journalist and former host, *7.30 Report*

'Crown: Playing in the Shadows *is an illuminating and important read. It contains important lessons for anyone concerned with the organisational health of organisations, be that businesses, government agencies or, indeed political parties. The book takes the reader on a journey. It raises issues and questions that are crucial to creating and maintaining healthy organisational cultures, practices and behaviours. Unfortunately, there is a strong tendency to assume that organisational culture is the responsibility of others (the other often being human resources). The other assumption is that leaders shape culture. The other assumptions that colour how culture is viewed are that it's shaped by leadership it 'just' evolves. How many times have you heard people say it's just the way things are around here? Everyone in an organisation shapes the culture and every one of those assumptions are, in fact, paralysing. They combine to stop people from actually doing anything about problems. They literally set the stage for shadow games. Everyone becomes an actor in a game none of them actually authored.'*

Steve Davies, organisational behaviour and information technology expert

'Comprehensively detailed, Tom Ravlic's captivating take on the Crown saga takes you into the pit of the casino business. Money, power and 'problems' collide as the company's sins come back to haunt it.'

Daniel Ziffer, ABC business news presenter, author

A Wunch of Bankers: A year in the Hayne Royal Commission

'Again, Ravlic has been true to form. He has expertly crafted a thorough, analytical account of the events previously sensationalised from East to West Coast. With an increased focus on trust, ethics and the role of regulators in all professions, this is a must read within the same battlefield as Enron: The Smartest Guys in the Room that happened decades earlier.'

Lisa Greig, tax trainer and lecturer, Holmesglen

'It's a great read, and very impressive in its scope, as well as the perceptiveness of the analysis.'

Senior regulatory officer

DEDICATION

Dr David Alexander McCredie AM (1926–2020).

He was the paediatric nephrologist at the Royal Children's' Hospital, Melbourne, that saved my life when I was an infant diagnosed with a rare disorder.

His example should remind all of us to aspire to do good.
Never forgotten. Eternally grateful.

Published by:
Wilkinson Publishing Pty Ltd
ACN 006 042 173
PO Box 24135
Melbourne, Vic 3001
Ph: 03 9654 5446
enquiries@wilkinsonpublishing.com.au
www.wilkinsonpublishing.com.au

Title: Crown Playing in the Shadows

ISBN: 9781925927962

eBook ISBN: 9781922810182

A catalogue record of this book is available from the National Library of Australia.

Design by Spike Creative Pty Ltd
Ph: (03) 9427 9500
spikecreative.com.au

Printed and bound in Australia by Griffin Press, a part of Ovato.

CONTENTS

FOREWORD

Australia has always had a love affair with gambling, stretching way back to our diggers playing 'two up' in both world wars.

Racehorses like Phar Lap, Winx and Black Caviar bind a nation. Then of course, you have the casinos, which are a modern-day phenomenon, but equally as popular.

And with all things that come down to money, the susceptibility for illegality is clear and obvious.

That's why gaming regulators are so strict—and clearly they've been working overtime in recent years, tracking the shenanigans of Australian gambling houses.

Tom Ravlic's new opus, *Crown: Playing in the Shadows*, details exactly what went down at one of the world's biggest casino operations, once headed up by Aussie family royalty, James Packer.

Ravlic explores the links on the way Crown enticed its high-roller clientele, especially the Chinese.

This placed Crown and its employees firmly in the sights of Chinese authorities, who were unhappy with Crown's modus operandi. The arrest of 19 Crown staff followed in 2016.

'Attempts to get a hook into the wallets of high worth Chinese players was always likely to rile Chinese authorities,' Ravlic wrote. 'They were playing with fire.'

Crown: Playing in the Shadows gives a remarkable insight into the rarefied atmosphere of high stakes casino gambling.

It is a terrific read.

Peter Gleeson

Queensland Editor, Sky News Australia

INTRODUCTION

Gambling is an enjoyable pursuit for many Australians. As much as possible, policy should aim to preserve the benefits, while targeting measures at gamblers facing significant risks or harm.

Productivity Commission Inquiry on Gambling, February 2010

The great historian, Russell Ward, writing in 1958, said there is a wealth of testimony to the passion for gambling. Perhaps this passion might explain, at least in part, why Australians have a distinctly liberal and egalitarian gambling culture.

Ray Finkelstein, Royal Commissioner

How did Crown find itself in this position? What caused the Crown Group to stray so far from its aspirations and the expectations of the community? What lessons can be drawn from Crown's experience?

Adrian Finanzio, Counsel Assisting the
Finkelstein Royal Commission

Hollywood has a habit of highlighting the seediest, most sensational, and controversial aspects of the running of casino businesses and the fascination with what goes on in darkened corners of gambling establishments is easy to understand. There is a curiosity with the rogues' gallery of ugly characters and the way in which people living in that parallel universe known as organised crime govern themselves and corrupt others for a buck or two or many millions along the way. Curiosity is further aroused when bad actors carry their crookedness into a legitimate business, attach themselves like a leech and attempt to bleed a business enough so that there is a bit left over for the next time they come collecting for whatever dark motivation takes their fancy. Protection with muscle, money laundering, gambling and other vices are woven through narratives that seek to entice a viewer to escape into a world other than their own for a little time.

A classic of the genre is the nineties' gangster flick aptly named *Casino* that takes a part of the life story of Frank 'lefty' Rosenthal, a renowned sports gambling identity and an administrator of four casinos on the part of the mafia in Las Vegas, and turns it into what amounts to a cinema goer's speed date with all of the sordid themes linked to the corruption of morals, organised crime rule, and mob violence. Some patrons to the Tangiers, a fictionalised casino said to resemble the Stardust, were dealt with violently by mafia associates of Sam Rothstein, a character based on Rosenthal and played by Robert de Niro, who became aware some folks decided to try and trick the house. Two of those mafia associates wind up getting killed themselves by mobsters because they were hotheads deemed much too hot to handle by the crooks let alone being too hot to handle for people outside the mob life. Money laundering, murder, infidelity, and an attempt to kill Rothstein himself using a car bomb are crammed into a runtime just short of three hours. It is enough time to sketch out characters, build tension, spill blood, and then resolve the story arc. It is, after all, entertainment.

Movie directors are fortunate that they are not charged with the task of solving societal problems in the same way as judges, magistrates, politicians, and—in the recent case of Australia's Crown casino network—royal commissioners. Reality bites when senior legal eagles are asked to take a close look at why a gambling enterprise, which lies at the centre of an Australian passion for a flutter irrespective of whether it is at a race, Saturday night lotto two-up on Anzac Day, winds up with a collection of curious problems. Figures such as Ray Finkelstein, the veteran jurist with 40 years at the bar under his belt in a career that also boasts appointments to various tribunals including the Federal Court, and Patricia Bergin, a respected jurist who has helmed various government inquiries, were tasked with looking at the way a widely reported case study of a dysfunctional corporation with serious governance and accountability issues failed to meet obligations. Both of those inquiries, which reported at different times during 2021, also considered what Crown Resorts could do to reengineer itself into an operation that works within the laws and regulations. A further inquiry into the gambling and entertainment giant was opened up in Western Australia and that remained running as Crown's year of reckoning before two inquiries and intense media scrutiny came to an end.

The task of each of the presiding officials and their legal teams was complex and challenging as it required them to balance the various elements at play in the running of Crown's casino properties in both Victoria and Western Australia and the seedier side of the operations that were reported on extensively in the media and drilled down into during the various public hearings. Consider the employment of entertainment, gaming, bar staff, maintenance teams, and administration staff that can come to many thousands of people alone. Casinos have various retail outlets, hotels, restaurants, entertainment venues such as concert venues and cinemas that would also employ chefs, sommeliers, waiters and waitresses, and the administration teams that are naturally required to keep the operations running. What happens to the enterprises, their owners, and the employees of these business that trade in the shadow of the casino. Their business depends on their being traffic coming in and out of a building housing what is without question a high-class gambling den. A Victorian government media release estimated that allowing Crown to trade on even though the Finkelstein deep dive into the listed corporation's affairs found them unfit to hold a license based on their activities prior to changes on their governing board and management changes would save about 12,000 jobs.

There is also the issue of gambling taxes, which Crown Casino was found to have dodged and later began to repay, and the amount of money that governments draw from gaming and gambling enterprises that winds up equalling billions of dollars contributed to state revenue in the same way as taxes on alcohol and tobacco contribute to the national coffers. Those funds are then used in part to pay for educational campaigns to get people to be responsible when they gamble. Programs of this nature are extensive and are also associated with research that looks at the nature of problem gambling and how gambling impacts on various demographics. This research by organisations such as the Victorian Responsible Gambling Foundation is important in order for a government to understand how best to deal with problem gambling that exists in some pockets of society while at the same time allowing for the operation of a casino and, frankly, any business that has some kind of games of chance.

Social refuge

Casinos and similar venues that have gaming or gambling facilities provide places for individuals of groups to visit and have a shared social experience. They fill a gap that might have been left through the inevitable loss of friends and loved ones as life's journey has gone on. Respondents to a study on factors that shape the gambling attitudes of older Victorian adults published in February 2020 by the Victorian Responsible Gambling Foundation told researchers they attended the gambling venues for both gambling and non-gambling activities. The reasons for attending such venues varied but a predominant reason was to be in the company of others especially in circumstances where a person's network of friends and family has grown smaller.

A female respondent to the study's researchers said attending a gambling venue means that you could engage with other people. 'The thing is, if you're sitting home on your own for maybe a whole weekend or three or four days with no contact and you just think I've just got to get out,' she said. 'So you go somewhere where there's going to be people. And even while you're playing the pokies you might talk to the lady or the gentleman next to you or whatever and you don't feel isolated when you're in an area where there's other people.' A male respondent to the same study said that he played electronic gaming machines when he dropped by to play bowls at the local bowls club. 'I only play when I come to bowls club. You know, I'll just have a few games I might do three games or something, and that about it. Just breaks a bit of boredom,' he said. There are also people that go there with friends, but they have a limit they are prepared to fritter away on entertainment. 'I only go there for entertainment with my friend, but we always have a limit,' a female respondent said. 'That's all. I go there, if I lost then there's nothing wrong because I know I have the limit and if I won that's good for me.'

The same study also found that people gambling at particular venues are pretty well clued up about the way in which venues want to keep them engaged with pushing buttons. 'These participants perceived that venues encouraged the extended use of machines through the provision of food and drinks while in the gaming area and attempted to draw older people into gambling venues to play the machines through venue vouchers and rewards,' the study says. A female respondent said that the staff at venues paid particular attention to their needs if they were gambling. 'They will come up, they will get you your drinks, they will bring you food, and they're really encouraging. So you've got to be strong to fight against it,' the respondent told researchers. Another female respondent observed that each machine they encountered provided the possibility of different returns. 'You'll probably get, say, free spins, or something like that,' she said. 'Because when you get free spins, you often get the bonuses, and they pay well. The ordinary just everyday symbols, three rarely pays very much in a five-line one. All machines differ. They're all different.' A male participant in the study confirmed to researchers that people understood that it was likely they would lose more than they would win on an electronic gaming machine. 'Well, they're set up not to win. That's for sure,' he said. 'Now and then you might have a little win, but you come back the next time, and you're going to lose it.'

There are studies that look at the problematic issue of gambling addiction that can create problems for individuals, partners or spouses and immediate families, and the general network they have around them. It is a field that is tilled regularly given the government funding provided for the research into gambling problems in order for health, law enforcement, and other organisations to understand precisely the nature of problems and possible solutions. There are groups that lobby against gambling establishments such as casinos with legitimate concerns, but a question that must also be kept in mind is what obsession or craze will somebody hooked on gambling adopt if gambling is unavailable to them?

Casino as crook magnets

Any gambling enterprise will be a target for crooked characters who have money they want to filter into respectable channels by laundering it via a gaming or gambling venue. Australian venues are not immune from the activities of money launderers with media reports and official inquiries showing that organised groups of players going into poker machine venues in New South Wales as well as the multiple inquiries into the operations of the various Crown Resorts venues that attracted eyeballs to live streams and dominated headlines. Casinos are recognised worldwide as venues that attract those with illicit gains and organisations such as the Financial Action Task Force (FATF). This global body seeks to minimise the occurrence of money laundering and terrorism financing across the globe and have sought to provide guidance to governments, financial institutions and other bodies on how to implement what the FATF calls a risk-based approach to dealing with money laundering in casinos and gaming institutions. Guidance was issued in 2008 by the FATF setting out the kinds of factors that jurisdictions need to keep in mind when assess the likelihood of money laundering and terrorism financing. It refers to the need to analyse the various kinds of risk factors that may be associated with the features of gambling operations that include but are not limited to electronic gaming machines, geographical location of a venue, and the kinds of customers the gambling venue attracts. Are most of the customers locals? What percentage of gamblers visiting a venue are actually tourists or people brought to the venue as a part of organised casino tours that are often termed 'junkets'. Each of these factors featured in one form or another during the examination of the Crown heavyweights and other assorted characters during the Finkelstein-led royal commission and the two other inquiries that have been run into the listed company's fitness to run a gambling enterprise.

Breaking the laws of other countries

What was also curious about the Crown operation is that they went out of their way to attempt to secure business in China and other countries within the region. This placed Crown and its employees squarely in the sights of the Chinese authorities that were unhappy with the attempt by Crown to try and hoover up more cash into its coffers by seducing potential gamblers to drop in to visit Melbourne. The arrest of 19 Crown staff followed in October 2016 and this then resulted 16 of those staff members getting time behind bars. Attempts to get a hook into the wallets of high worth Chinese players was always likely to rile Chinese authorities. Crown executives knew that the remit set for their staffers was playing with fire. What did Crown do in other jurisdictions when their Chinese team felt the full weight of the Chinese law? Staff members promoting Crown's gambling gig in Melbourne to people in Indonesia, Malaysia, Taiwan, and Singapore were basically left to continue promoting the casino business even though it was entirely plausible that the same laws that saw their staff imprisoned in China existed in those jurisdictions.

This is not the only way in which Crown sought to muck about with the rules of a foreign jurisdiction. The company seemed quite willing to provide wealthy Chinese clients with a funnel into which they could put their hard-earned dough so they could gamble at Crown in Australia. There were bank accounts for two Crown subsidiaries that were set up in order to have an intermediate destination for those funds before they made their way to their ultimate destination. The Bergin Report found that banks that had Crown as a client did whatever they could to shut bank accounts down when it became apparent what the gambling concern was doing. The banks were playing whack-a-mole and Crown was trying desperately to stay just a little ahead. It is a rather ironic situation given that another prominent inquiry into misconduct in the financial services sector had spent a full year eviscerating the banking and financial services sector for inappropriate behaviour that resulted in losses to clients. The banks that sought to shut down the accounts Crown used to provide its customers with a degree of privacy were doing the right thing.

Curious bedfellows

A further concern that has caused official inquiries to reflect on Crown's fitness to hold casino licenses in several jurisdictions is the episode involving Melco Resorts and Entertainment in 2019. A company owned by James Packer that had 46 per cent of Crown Resort shares cut a deal with Melco Resorts and Entertainment so that Melco would have a 19.9 per cent stake in Crown Resorts. There was just little problem with that scenario given that Crown had undertaken to ensure that Stanley Ho, an individual suspected of links to organised crime, and his associates had no interest in casinos. Eyebrows were raised at the fact Ho's son Lawrence had a substantial interest in Melco. Did that relationship between Ho and his son mean that the deal Crown cut with Melco breach the agreement with the authorities in New South Wales? The Bergin inquiry found that the Melco deal did not breach agreements. This did not save Crown nor its largest shareholder from scalpels of the Bergin Inquiry and the finding of unsuitability. The Packer involvement in Crown was set to wrap up with a takeover of the gambling and entertainment play by private equity firm, Blackstone. Blackstone's showing of love for Crown Resorts was announced on Valentine's Day, 2022, and wrapped up in that was a cash offer for shares that Crown directors said was a good deal for shareholders.

Governance and culture

None of these kinds of illicit activities that occurred in the shadows and later emerged like some rash or skin blemish took place without the knowledge of certain managers within the business. The degree of organisation involved, for example, to set up bank accounts to park money transferred to Crown by prospective Chinese clients that was later transferred to Crown itself is not small. It requires people within the structure being involved in making these things happen. The laundering of funds, the blacking out of gaming buttons on electronic gaming machines to lure punters to use a more expensive option, and the running of junkets for overseas high worth fritters of funds all need to take place with some kind of coordination and planning. The question always is what and when those in charge of governance—ultimately the board of an entity—knew about the activities that were being undertaken in their name and the name of shareholders. A further issue that always requires exploration in these circumstances is how great a role is played by incentives to push an entity towards reporting an attractive result to the financial markets. This is an issue that is not unique to the gambling sector but a question that is equally relevant in other types of businesses that have seen taxpayer funds given to royal commissions designed to see what profit motives do to organisations that deal with vulnerable cohorts. Both the banking royal commission and the royal commission into the aged care sector revealed significant problems. The banking royal commission featured a prominent case study of an addicted gambler that was given increases of credit over time despite telling the relevant bank that he had a gambling problem. Profit took precedence over pastoral care and corporate responsibility in that case. Another royal commission looked at aged care and there again was an example of profit driven institutions providing the bare minimum or residents The three inquiries that have been conducted into Crown reveal similar issues that arose in the casino sector. There is an ongoing inquiry into Star City in News South Wales that was still ongoing at the time of writing that has revealed similar behaviour.

Risk management rather than risk avoidance

There are various ideas that were thrown up for how the nasties that crop up in the running of casinos can be managed during the research of this book. One of those was the notion of restricting the shareholding in gambling enterprises, which might solve aspects of governance that relate to control of a corporation and potentially result in a different dynamic on the board of directors. That may flow through in dealing with cultural issues in an organisation because the difference in a board's composition may impact on the way a chief executive deals with operational divisions of a company. Another suggestion thrown up during the research was breaking the corporation up into smaller components and having different boards run companies that were permitted under law to have only one casino. It could increase competition in the gaming sector but such a suggestion could also multiply the avenues for organised crime influence to manifest itself. Anyone desperate enough to launder ill-gotten gains will find a forum for this over time.

Each of these suggestions might have advantages in shaking up a corporate structure and changing aspects of operations in order to refresh the way things are looked at by a board of directors, senior management, and the teams that work below them. What they don't do is remove the reality that organised crime cosies up to it because of the ease with which money can be pushed through machines and via other games played in those venues. Managing the behaviour of staff members involved in the handling of funds to avoid ethical and legal breaches becomes important. Ensuring laws, regulations, and internal policies designed to minimise harm to gamblers and, frankly, harm to the reputation of the organisation itself over time are enforced goes without saying. Terminating the employment of individuals that are engaged in inappropriate activities is equally critical so a clear ethical direction for the organisation is set. Consequences must exist for poor behaviour otherwise other people might be tempted to tinker with darkness.

Gambling enterprises have more moving parts than a grandfather clock, and when the conduct of any aspect of the operations of a casino is outside acceptable standards and against the law the entire enterprise risks regulatory intervention, political interference, poking and prodding by judicial figures, media attention, and, of course, reputational damage. What needs to be remembered when people examine the issues beyond the headlines is that these are entertainment venues that employ people, provide people with amusement, and also provide governments with the ability to provide services to assist with problem gambling through the collection of taxes. Then there is the problem of illicit gambling, which the Productivity Commission referred to in its 2010 report on the gambling sector in Australia, if gambling was not conducted in a regulated environment. 'Prohibition would erode people's freedom and would risk the criminality and corruption associated with the provision of illicit gambling,' the Productivity Commission said. 'This provides the rationale for one of the most important policy stances of government in relation to gambling—simply allowing it to be legally supplied'. Allowing people to have fun while attempting to manage the risks involved is key. You can bet a few bob on any government not wanting to encourage the rise of the next Al Capone.

THE GAMBLING SECTOR: A THUMBNAIL SKETCH

Gambling has been a feature of Australian society and its economy since the arrival of the First Fleet. But even by Australian standards, the recent proliferation of gambling opportunities and the growth in the gambling industries have been remarkable.

Productivity Commission report into
Australia's Gambling Industries,1999

They say one of the common features is that people are chasing losses because they think that there's a win around the corner, but of course the way the machines operate, it just isn't like that.

Nick Xenophon, lawyer and former Senator of the
Australian Parliament, 2010

It took until 1999 for Australians to get what was touted by then Prime Minister John Howard as the first comprehensive overview of the gambling sector in Australia. Howard's media release launching the two-volume report by the Productivity Commission noted the eternal conundrum faced by government when dealing with problem gambling and allowing Australians to enjoy fun playing games of chance. 'The challenge for all governments in Australia is to find a response which balances the undoubted right of individual Australians to gamble if they wish with the ongoing responsibility of governments for overall community welfare,' Howard said. The then Prime Minister noted that he was concerned about the increase in problem gambling reflected by the report with his 16 December 1999 media release stating that the report found that at that time 290,000 were problem gamblers and that problem gamblers accounted for $3 billion in annual losses. 'This is disastrous not only for these problem gamblers, but also for the estimate 1.5 million people they directly affect as a result of bankruptcy, divorce, suicide, and lost time at work.' Howard used the launch to tell Australians that the government would be adopting the recommendation to set up a ministerial council on gambling that would aim to deal with issues of problem gambling as well as the establishment of an advisory body to assist with advice to ministers regarding emerging trends in problem gambling.

The comprehensive review came at a time when Australia had seen a growth in casinos that first began with the Wrest Point Casino in Tasmania in 1973. Wrest Point was followed by SkyCity Darwin in 1979. SkyCity Darwin would later become know as Mindil Beach Casino Resort. The time between the establishment of new casinos began to get shorter during the 1980s with six casinos getting approval. Lasseters opened up in Alice Springs in 1981, Country Club Tasmania opened in Launceston in 1982. Adelaide's SkyCity flung its doors open in 1985 as did Burswood Entertainment Complex in Perth and Conrad Jupiters on the Gold Coast. Townsville got its own Jupiters' venue with Jupiters hotel and casino opening in 1986.

It was not until the next decade that two of Australia's most populated states got casinos with Crown Melbourne opening its doors in 1994 and Star City Sydney kicked off its operations in 1995. Other casinos established during the 1990s included Casino Canberra, which opened in 1992, Conrad Treasury Casino started in 1995, and the

Reef Hotel Casino was opened in 1996. Each of these establishments came with the novelty of a new place for entertainment but it's also ushered in a period where electronic gaming machines or—as they are colloquially known, the pokies—started to get attention as being the antichrist when it came to the problem gambling.

Casinos over time attracted people that were prepared to throw a bit more money around that the average person on the street and the VIP segment of the market, the high roller and high-profile gamblers, became more significant over the years. The key casinos the VIP market was critical for were Crown Melbourne, Crown Perth, The Star Sydney, The Star Gold Coast. The special gambler market was also focused on by Darwin's Mindil Beach Casino Resort and also The Treasury in Brisbane. This VIP market would bring an intense focus on the gambling marketplace because it would later be synonymous with the bringing in people keen to launder funds irrespective of whether they were organised crime figures or just rich people wanting their money out of their home country to play games at an overseas venue.

Polarisation of discourse on gambling

The Productivity Commission was tasked to provide an overview of the gambling sector in Australia when it became apparent that discussions about the merits and demerits of gambling of various kinds were being had in a vacuum at a time when the gambling sector had increased exponentially given the growth in gambling products and the increased presence of casinos across Australia. How do you measure problems in a specific area if nobody has done a substantive piece of work that actually lays out landscape that is being disputed, debated, disagreed or agreed upon by protagonists? How does anybody involved in the tussle over the gambling industry know precisely what they are talking about, arguing over, or trying to solve if they are operating in the absence of an agreed set of facts about the state of play in the gambling sector? Industry advocates would argue for the sector and also seek to persuade decision makers in government that the sector provides economic benefits, entertainment to the punters that wander into establishments, and that those same punters should be to exercise the freedom to choose to gamble. Opponents of gambling in the other corner of this intellectual bout would argue that the social costs of gambling—homelessness, bankruptcy, addiction—outweigh any benefits. The intricate mosaic assembled by the Productivity Commission across a three-volume report, which was accompanied by a report summary, provided a more informed basis for balanced national discourse on how the gambling sector both benefits and negatively impacts the broader community.

State of gambling industry in 1999

The Productivity Commission's landmark work emerged at a time when Australia had started to see a broadening of the impact gambling was having across the Australian community. This is because of the growth in several sectors that had begun to be available for punters because of legalisation. It is important to note at the outset that ten to 15 years prior to 1999 report lotteries and betting on the races were the only legal forms of gambling. Growth in the gambling sector came from the establishment of casinos and the growing presence of poker machines, different lottery products starting to take hold, sports betting emerging and an early form of internet gambling. Gambling had also become more accessible in suburban locations and along with accessibility came forms of gambling that were much quicker such as poker machines. These machines would result in in higher spends on gambling over time because of the faster game play. Various government run gambling bodies were also privatised and this meant the influence of commercial objectives was more likely to come into play as would the greater advertising of the gambling businesses intended to turn a profit.

Gamblers back in 1997-98 were said to have spent or lost—depending on your perspective—more than $11 billion with $3.5 billion of that paid out in taxes from a turnover of $95 billion. The Productivity Commission said that the expenditure was double the amount spent a decade earlier and that the advent of new kinds of gambling did not necessarily mean that other parts of the sector suffered. Gaming machines accounted for 52 per cent of expenditure in 1997–98 outside casinos, for example, when they were only 29 per cent in 1987-88. 'While gaming machines' share of total gambling expenditure has risen, its growth appears not to have displaced other gambling modes—which have largely maintained their previous growth trends—but rather has been at the expense of other consumption items or saving (future consumption),' the report said. There were 7000 businesses at that time that provided gambling related services across the country with the number being made up of 13 casinos, 2888 pubs, 2408 clubs and the balance is made up of other enterprises and lotteries. Employment in the gambling sector was significant with the 1999 report stating that there were more than 37,000 people employed in businesses where the key purpose was gambling with about 20,000 of those people being employed in casinos across Australia. Venues such as clubs, pubs, taverns, and bars where gambling was present but not the primary activity employed at least 120,000 people. Gambling taxation nearly doubled during the 1997-98 financial year and it came close to representing 12 per cent of the tax take that wound up in state and territory coffers.

The flip side of the coin—the problems caused by gambling—also received attention in this inaugural report with an estimate of 290,000 people having what was regarded by the 1999 report's authors as having a gambling problem. That total of 290,000 is made up of 130,000 Australians that were deemed to have severe gambling problems that may require professional help to stop and 160,000 people with moderate problems that the Productivity Commission said should be treated as an area of policy concern even if they did not require treatment for problem gambling. Individuals classified as problem gamblers made up 15 per cent of the regular gambling cohort and their slice of the spend in the gambling sector was around $3.5 billion. Average losses for a problem gambler at that time were $12,000 a year with other gamblers only losing about $650 a year in the late 1990s.

The gambling sector a decade later

Gambling was the subject of another Productivity Commission report in 2010 and the commission noted in its introduction that this particular deep dive into gambling is very different to the 1999 report A key reason for this is the fact there had been a decade for the gambling sector to grow and for parts of the market to develop further. 'Gaming industries, and particularly the EGM market, have now matured. And, while community concerns about gambling have remained, participation in gambling has decreased and expenditure growth has stagnated,' the report said. 'Moreover, new mediums for gambling are bringing new challenges for policy and new risks for consumers. Online gaming and wagering, as well as sports betting, have grown rapidly in prominence over the past decade (although they still constitute a small share of gambling expenditure).' The authors of this second report also noted that the 1999 report was prepared and released a t a time when some jurisdictions had introduced casinos for the first time as well as introduced poker machines into the community. Opening up these forms of gambling to the community during the late 1980s and throughout the 1990s caused disruption.

A decade is a long time between drinks. The commission's researchers noted that fewer people were aware of the way in which tax laws, competition rules, and regulation impacting the gambling sector than there are today. Greater weight has been given by various jurisdiction to the social harms of gambling following the first productivity commission report whereas, according to the 2010 report, there was a greater focus on developing the sector as well as ensuring governments were raising revenue from the gambling sector. Harm minimisation did not just take place in the form of people introducing policies on responsible gambling, Venues also found that taking a stand on banning smoking, caused gambling revenue to decline.

Advocates for the gambling sector were miffed that more space was not given to the benefits of the gambling sector in the second report. The Australasian Gaming Council gave the Productivity Commission a whack around the ears in its submission to the draft report. Industry representatives said it believed that the commission's researchers did not comply with terms of reference set for it by the Council of Australian Governments, but the Productivity Commission has the last laugh. The terms of references said the Commission could provide an updated version of the 1999 report but that was not what the Commission chose to do. It decided to look more intensely at policies aimed at achieving 'greater net benefits from gambling for Australians, not simply to reconstruct a static balance sheet of benefits and costs'. The previous report served as a foundation but the Commission went on to the serious business of reform rather than give different sides of the discourse equal space in the report for the sake of balance.

The 2010 gambling snapshot

People spent $19 billion on gambling products, which represents an increase from about $17 billion in 1998-99, and that in itself was a jump from the $7 billion in gambling spend in 1988–89. The impact of the growth of gambling across two decades is reflected in those figures. Spending on gambling increased overall but there was another trend highlighted in 2010. Households were spending less on gambling in 2008–09 (3.1 per cent) than they did in 1998–99 (3.9 per cent). Poker machines hoovered money out of people's pockets with $10.5 billion on poker machines operated by clubs and hotels but $1.4 billion on poker machines in casinos in 2008–09. Revenue from poker machines might have grown but this does not mean that that the venues in which the machines were played had it easy. Bans on smoking in venues meant there was a decline in revenue growth. There was no recovery to the levels of growth in the use of gaming machines that were reported when the 1999 report was released. 'The rate of growth in real gambling expenditure slowed during the 2000s. The five-year trend growth in real expenditure was less than 1 per cent in 2008–09, compared with over 10 per cent during the 1990s,' the Productivity Commission said. 'And, spending on gambling accounted for around 3.9 per cent of final consumption expenditure in 1999, compared to 3.1 per cent in 2008-09.'

Wagering such as the punters betting on horse racing did not change particularly much over two decades but sports wagering grew significantly. It made up 15 per cent of the total gambling spend while a bundle of others collectively known as lotteries, pools and keno made up 12 per cent of the total amount that was spent on gambling by punters. 'Lotteries and pools provide the majority of gambling tax revenue in Western Australia, and they comprise the second largest source of gambling tax revenue in all other jurisdictions except the Northern Territory,' the Productivity Commission. 'The considerable tax revenues associated with lotteries in various jurisdictions are in contrast to their relatively smaller share of gambling expenditure.'

The 2010 report did not reflect much in the way of information on online gaming. Those activities were illegal and not captured by the tax authorities, but the commission's researchers estimated that this less visible and less legal gambling past times made up four per cent of the total gambling spend in 2008-09. There are also differences in the way states and territories classified these forms of gambling. 'Tasmania categorises such expenditure as interactive gambling, while the Northern Territory categorises revenue from online bookmakers as either racing or sports betting,' the commission's report notes. 'Interactive (online) gambling services account for around 6 per cent of Tasmania's gambling tax revenue, which is more than in any other state or territory—largely reflecting the activities of the Betfair betting exchange which established operations in that state in 2006.'

The number of serious problem gamblers in the 2010 report was said to have be 115,000 with a further estimate of 280,000 people being what the report called gamblers at moderate risk. Electronic gaming or poker machines remained the highest risk way for people with a serious gambling problem to do their dough. Consider the fact that poker machines accounted for 62 per cent of total expenditure at the time while wagering represented 15 per cent of cash thrown at gambling and table games represented only seven per cent of expenditure. 'The risks of problem gambling increase significantly with the frequency of playing electronic gaming machines,' the report said 'The Commission estimates that among those who play weekly or more on gaming machines, around 15 per cent are problem gamblers with an additional 15 per cent at "moderate risk".' One of the reasons that they make up a high percentage of the spend on gambling is that they are not only accessible in casinos but also accessible in clubs and various other venues in the suburbs.

The more accessible the machines became over time, the more the punters in the burbs got themselves hooked, but this is nothing novel or new. Accessibility of machines in clubs in New South Wales first began to bob up in venues in the 1920s. Hotels struck trouble in the courts when machines began to operate in hotel premises and a full bench Supreme Court ruling declared them illegal. Clubs were able to continue to run the machines in their clubs in part because of the fact that the profits went to the clubs themselves rather than a machine owner. The regulation tightened during the 1930s.

That report also noted that there are a series of vulnerabilities that also need to be considered in the analysis of why and how people gravitate toward gaming machines. Some people believed that they could recover losses by playing more and that certain machines do what some gamblers call run 'hot' or 'cold'.

'The consequence of these faulty cognitions is that people make expenditure decisions based on significant underestimation of the price they are paying for the good,' the report's authors observed. 'People often have faulty beliefs, but most of these beliefs do not have the adverse consequences that can arise here.'

The other issue highlighted in this report and elsewhere at the time is that the speed at which games repeated themselves also created the sustained gambling as well as creating a climate where losses could be greater if someone glued themselves to their seat chasing a win.

Costs and benefits of gambling

Both of the Productivity Commission reports spent a significant amount of time examining what various submitters to the inquiries said were the costs and benefits of gambling with the more recent of the two reports offering estimates of the aggregate of the benefit from gambling in dollar terms. The Productivity Commission estimated that the tax revenue and enjoyment of gambling for people who would be classed as recreational gamblers was somewhere between $12.1 billion to $15.8 billion during 2008-09. Costs to problems gamblers, which is the flip side of the fun equation, ranged from $4.7 billion and $8.4 billion. The net benefit estimated by the Productivity Commission was somewhere between $3.7 and $11.1 billion. The commission's researchers said that benefits could have been greater if the government reduced costs through prevention and harm minimisation policies.

Casinos and hotels provided benefits to the community thought funding for community and sporting groups as well as charities. The 2010 report said that contributions of this kind from casinos came to $10.9 million with $4.6 million went to sporting and cultural events and $1.8 million went to charitable institutions. Another benefit provided to the community by casinos was the in-kind donation of venue space for the hosting of fundraising events. A report prepared by The Allen Consulting Group for the Australian Casino Association as part of the industry body's materials presented to the commission observed that organisations such as the Flinders Medical Centre Foundation, Cancer Council Queensland, the Salvation Army, Make a Wish Foundation and Westmead Children's Hospital. Hotels with gaming facilities had a similar focus on contributing to community groups, sporting teams, religious groups and other associations. A study conducted by PricewaterhouseCoopers on the hotel sector found that donations and fundraising for community groups by hotels was more likely to occur if the hotel had poker machines as a part of its operation. 'The largest average amount provided was in relation to sporting groups (in addition to sporting groups being the most common recipients of support),' the PricewaterhouseCoopers report prepared for the Australian Hotels Association. 'Of those providing support, $8,792 per hotel was provided. In relation to community groups, the average level of support was $4,733.' The PricewaterhouseCoopers report estimated that the various community groups, sporting clubs, and charities received $75 million from the hotels.

Almost 200 submissions received by the commission's inquiry team for the 2010 report came from clubs that described the way in which their groups operated within their communities. Leagues Clubs Australia told the commission that clubs play a part in growing rugby league across New South Wales and Queensland. 'Our members also provide similar substantial support for a wide range of other sporting activities — rugby union, soccer, cricket, hockey, netball, swimming, athletics, cycling, tennis, Australian rules, and a number of indoor sports,' the Leagues Club Australia submission said. The clubs also provide support for other groups within their communities. Recreational, Sports and Aquatic Club highlighted its work as a registered charity in sport, recreation, carer support and personal development activities for disabled people in 10 local government areas in Sydney. 'RSL Victorian Branch said they were a "home away from home" for some of their members. It was also noted that clubs are often the focal point of towns and surrounding areas in regional and rural areas,' the Productivity Commission said.

Community assistance has always been a feature in various kinds of gambling and lottery services. Gambling and lotteries also have had other purposes in Australia's history. One notable example is the Golden Casket Art Union that was started by a group called the Queensland Patriot Committee in 1916 that asked the government to permit it to start a lottery that would benefit a soldier repatriation fund. It succeeded in getting permission and the committee raised 60,000 pounds for those that were victims of the First World War. The Golden Casket Art Union was later controlled by the government as it was seen as a source of revenue. The Golden Casket was a consistent and substantial kicker to government coffers. 'Other states introduced their own lotteries and permitted charitable organisations to conduct minor gaming such as bingo, raffles and art unions,' the 1999 report on the gaming sector said. 'By the 1930s lotteries and minor gaming were legitimised throughout Australia and the association with welfare gave gambling a new respectability.'

Contemporary data on losses in gambling

The data on the benefits and detriments of gambling in the two Productivity Commission reports that cover the entire sector reflect the state of the gambling sector at the time those reports were publishing. More contemporary data available from the Australian Institute of Health and Welfare estimates that Australian gamblers and punters frittered away about $25 billion on legal forms of gambling during the 2018-19 financial year. Research reported by the Institute notes the Victoria's social cost of gambling was thought to be around $7 billion. Costs of social gambling include financial problems, psychological costs, impact of gambling on personal, professional and family relationship.

About 6.5 million people that are aged 18 and over spent money in a typical month in 2018 on gambling, according to the Household, Income and Labour Dynamics in Australia. This represents a drop in the number of people involved that were involved in gambling since 2015. There were 6.8 million Australians engaged in gambling in 2015. There were marked changes in the frequency with which Australians were playing certain games. Lotto and lottery games, instant scratch tickets and poker machines were all gambling activities that saw a decline in spending by Australians. Lotto and lottery games, for example, fell from expenditure that hit 30 per cent in 2015 to 27 per cent in 2018. A more controversial form of gaming, pokier machines or electronic gaming, fell from 8.1 per cent in 2015 to7.4 per cent in 2018. Betting on sports and horse or dog racing grew with betting on horse and dog races jumping from 5.6 per cent in 2015 up to 6.2 per cent in

2018. Sports betting has gone up to 4.6 per cent in 2018 from 3.3 per cent in 2015.

A total number of Australian adults that gambled dropped from 39 per cent in 2015 to 35.2 per cent in 2018. Males continued to gamble more than women even though the total of men and women gambling dropped in 2018. Men made up 43.1 per cent of gamblers in 2015 but this number went down in to 39.6 per cent in 2018. The total of women that gambled in 2018 was 31 per cent. This was a decline in the number of female gamblers from the 35 per cent reported in 2015. Adults most likely to gamble were aged 55 and over with 49.2 percent of adults that were 55 years of age or above gambling in 2015 with gamblers in that age group dropping down to 46.7 per cent.

Gambling during the COVID-19 pandemic

The coronavirus pandemic saw a battery of health orders issued in Australia that meant gambling at casinos was generally not permitted given concerns about the spread of the virus in indoor entertainment, dining, and other venues. A study published by the Australian Gambling Research Centre titled Gambling in Australia during COVID-19, published in October 2020, found that gambling behaviours changed. A survey of more than 2,000 people conducted in June-July 2020 explored what gamblers responding to researchers did to gamble before the pandemic hit and what happened when the opportunity to gamble on certain kinds of sports vanished because of the suspension of international and national sporting contests due to the pandemic.

The researchers found that 79 per cent of respondents said they gambled at least once a week during the 12 months prior to the survey taking place and that under 30 per cent of participants said they gambled at least four—if not more—times during that period. Gambling on horse racing before the pandemic hit and during remained steady at 57 per cent, according to the researchers. Gambling on sports experienced a minor drop from 46 per cent prior to the pandemic to 45 per cent once the pandemic began to take hold. Lotto dropped from 41 per cent before the onset of COVID 19 to 38 per cent and greyhound racing experienced a slight jump from 35 per cent to 37 per cent once the pandemic took hold. There were, however, some major changes in gambling habits for those that were a part of the research project. Players of electronic gaming machines or pokies were forced to go cold turkey when the virus appeared and the research figures show a drop from 35 per cent to 14 per cent. Researchers found that instant scratch tickets' appeal fell from 13 per cent before the plague to 10 per cent with keno experiencing a more dramatic fall from 12 per cent before restrictions slowed the gambling business to six per cent. It was inevitable that certain games at casinos would experience a significant fall in patronage. Table games in casinos dropped from 10 per cent to three per cent.

The study provided anecdotes from people who saw their gambling habits change during the pandemic. One of the respondents to the survey told researchers that they became even more partial to gambling during the pandemic. 'I've been thinking to myself that COVID has accelerated my gambling and that of my friends. Every weekend we share our bets for each game of the day and discuss them as they happen,' a male respondent aged 27 told researchers. 'As silly as it sounds, it's brought us closer somewhat, a distraction and something to do—but all of my friendship group have accelerated gambling, and some have started for the first time during COVID.' Another male respondent turned 18 when during the first part of the pandemic. He said he spent time in isolation gambling. A 59-year old female respondent told researchers she had spent more money on her mobile betting application during the pandemic. Other respondents remarked how much healthier their bank account looked while they were unable to leave home to play bingo or the gaming machines at a casino or another venue.

Australia and gambling history

The Productivity Commission's reports from 1999 and 2010 acknowledged the long history of gambling as a past time in Australia with the earliest games of chance or wagering making their way as a part of the influx of European settlement with influence that can be traced from Britain, Asia and the European continent. The various reviews into Crown Casino and other gambling establishment over the past two decades are an acknowledgement of the role gambling and wagering in its various forms plays in the Australian community. What the different reviews into Australian casinos also emphasise the need for this legal form of entertainment to be run as cleanly, legally, and fairly as possible. The more contemporary reviews into Crown Casino found that the casinos operating under the banner of Crown Resorts were sprung running operations that were not as clean or as legally compliant as required under law.

AN OPENING ADDRESS

Gambling has significant benefits. The industry generates substantial income and employs many people. Gambling taxation provides a significant and growing proportion of State revenue. It currently accounts for about 12 per cent of State-generated taxes.

Ray Finkelstein, the royal commissioner

Ray Finkelstein found himself in an unenviable position at the start of his inquiry into the operations of Crown. The Bergin Report had lobbed on the tables of the parliament in New South Wales with the finding that Crown was unfit to hold a license to run a casino in Sydney that was intended for the Barangaroo site and was in some respects a hard act to follow. It would be difficult for Finkelstein to conclude differently on issues given that much of the evidence considered by Bergin would be considered by him. Finkelstein's inquiry would need to take note of the Bergin findings while also trying to navigate its way through a large corporate operation, its internal workings and policies, and to quiz the right people in order to get sufficient evidence to come to an authoritative view on what should happen with Crown and its license.

Bergin's observations on persistent laundering of funds through subsidiaries, the disregard for the welfare of staff in a jurisdiction where selling access to gambling facilities in Australia was unwelcome, and junket operations that had links with Chinese triads as well as other criminal groups were noted in the first address delivered by Finkelstein. He acknowledged the fact there was an inevitable overlap on the issues he needed to consider and the material that the Bergin inquiry trawled through. Finkelstein wrote to Crown to test whether the company accepted the Bergin Inquiry's conclusions on its propriety and fitness to hold the license. He did this to try to avoid opening up the same issues during his poke through the corporate innards of the gambling if in fact there was no need to do so. His first letter to Crown asking whether they company accepted what the Bergin Inquiry found was, according to Finkelstein, 'a little equivocal'. 'The Crown companies do not accept, in terms, the findings made by Commissioner Bergin which I have earlier read out. The disagreement, however, may not be material,' Finkelstein observed. 'The aspect of the findings to which objection seems to be taken goes to the deliberateness or wilfulness of the conduct concerned.' The letter did note that the companies accepted that it was open for the Bergin Inquiry to conclude based on the evidence and testimony presented before it that Crown was not a suitable associate of the Sydney-based gaming venue. The letter received by Finkelstein from Crown did argue that Crown Melbourne is a suitable person to hold a license and that Crown Resorts should be considered suitable to associate with it. This is jargon that simply means that the companies should be considered able to run a casino enterprise together under the law. Crown argued that its reform program would clean things up and that the entities involved in the casino enterprise would emerge fit at the end. That was something Finkelstein would note much later.

Finkelstein's opening address provided the watchers of this particular courtroom drama early indications of what to expect as he trawled through the ethical and risk management mess that had been laid out in various forums. Money laundering was going to be an inevitable focus right from the outset given the key risks outline not just by the Bergin Inquiry, but by various inquiries into the gambling sector in Australia and overseas. The inquiry would also need to answer whether Crown was in breach of laws and regulations and also contractual agreements with the State. Thorny issues about the way in which the casino dealt with gambling addiction would also be considered.

Crown's lawyers were also approached by the counsel for the royal commission to provide access to legal advice that relates to issues that would be probed by Finkelstein and his colleagues. This raised the usual discussion about whether legal professional privilege would apply to documents that were being sought as exhibits but were also a part of legal matters that were active. Finkelstein said that the matter has a clear, obvious solution. I should point out that problems of this kind, no doubt, can be satisfactorily dealt with by confidentiality orders,' the royal commissioner said. 'Any person seeking particular protection for its documents should, in the first instance, raise that matter with the Commission's solicitors.' Legal professional privilege debates and any other tactics that delayed the production of documents to the royal commissioner and his team would 'not be tolerated', Finkelstein said.

Finkelstein's inquiry came after the Bergin inquiry in New South Wales had already reported in the first quarter of 2021. That inquiry that was in part prompted by the reportage in Nine Entertainment newspapers related to the way in which the Casino had been linked to organised crime influences and how the company treated employees asked to hawk Crown business. Bergin noted that threats posed by organised crime were complicated and they required the cooperation between information gathering, regulatory and law enforcement agencies as well as casinos themselves. 'It no doubt requires, amongst other things, the use of sophisticated and cutting-edge technology and practices to keep abreast of, and hopefully ahead of, what is happening in this area,' Bergin said in her opening statement on the 21 January 2020. Bergin's inquiry did not simply take a look at Crown as an organisation, but the effectiveness of the regulatory mechanisms used to regulate casinos in New South Wales. This was in order to examine whether any of the regulatory structures themselves create problems when it came to dealing with the prickly area of casino regulation. 'From a public interest perspective, it is important that if it be the case that the present structure and/or practices in place for the regulatory bodies of casinos within our jurisdiction and the capacity for sensible liaison and communication with and between the regulatory body, the law enforcement agencies and the casino operators do not facilitate or enable effective control of the risks that are presented by the operation of casinos in our society, then you will expect and the public will expect that a robust and equally sophisticated and cutting-edge approach will need to be adopted to ensure that there is capacity to effectively control those risks,' Bergin said.

The Western Australian Royal Commission into Crown's activities is chaired by another respected jurist for whom corporate collapses and governance failures are not novel. Neville Owen, the chairman of the royal commission into the failure of insurance group HIH in 2001, is at the helm of the royal commission looking at the operations of Crown. He is one of three commissioners that was selected to preside over the royal commission in the West with the other two being former judge Lindy Jenkins and Colin Murphy, Western Australia's former auditor-general. Owen's opening statement noted that the New South Wales and Victorian inquiries needed to form a part of the body of material considered by the Western Australian inquiry because the public interest was not served by people going over old ground that had already been explored in evidence by a previous inquiry into the same entity. The three inquiries were complimentary rather than competing and as such it made sense to not replicate work already done. What adds to the complexity of any examination of Crown and its affairs is that each state has its own regime for regulating gambling enterprises and those issues require an independent examination. Such are the wonders of the Australian federal system of government.

How and why did Finkelstein and his peers across two other states come to deal with problems within one of Australia's largest companies that had scored licenses to print money by running casinos across two states and hoping to run another? That requires a ride in a time machine to travel back to a period when having a casino in Victoria was a novel idea and allowing one to exist brought with it more problems than it would ever solve.

CAIN, KIRNER AND REGULATORY FROLICS

Whatever the historical derivation of the word 'casino' may be, I think that in 1983 it is taken to describe premises in which certain games of chance are played for stakes. The games vary considerably from country to country.

Xavier Connor, chair of the board of inquiry into casinos, 1983

I caution the House today that if we allow the government to carry on with its sudden rush of blood to the head to a gambling-led recovery - it has nothing to offer the manufacturing industry—we will find a completely uncoordinated gambling industry in this State.

Phil Honeywood, Victorian Liberal Party MP, May 1991

The road to three inquiries and allegations of breaches of multiple rules for Crown Casino began long before the notion of a palatial complex was even a glint in the eyes of any politician or corporate executive. This story begins back in the early 1980s with the election of the government of John Cain and the Australian Labor Party that turned to a respected jurist, Xavier Connor, to assess whether a casino should be introduced in the State of Victoria in the same way as gambling establishments were popping up around the rest of Australia. The same political party was still in government when they turned to the same man again on the same issue. Connor was asked to work out what might be the best way of introducing a casino into the state given the Labor government led at that stage by Joan Kirner and her administration wanted a casino in place. Victoria was a state without one of these establishments and both the government and opposition wanted to get a casino moving. The question for the second lap around the same topic was where and how rather than whether there ought to be a casino.

The first lap

Connor's first report to the Labor administration headed by then premier John Cain was about getting at the heart of whether Victoria should have a casino. His multiple volume report shows evidence of a careful, forensic, and thorough examination of various issues that the government of that day requested the respected jurist take a deep dive into. This report was the included feedback and material from all over the world and it examined different regulatory regimes and the complete box and dice when it came to coming to a view on whether the state was ready for a casino. The report also included chapters examining the kinds of establishments that could be contemplated by the Victorian government to meet what Connor saw was a moderate demand for casino gambling. 'They contributed in quite different ways from Lord Allen of Abbeydale, the present chairman of the Gaming Board for Great Britain to Father James Halley, the Parish Priest of a poor Puerto Rican parish in Atlantic City,' Connor said. 'Casino regulator officials, casino operators and their staffs at all the places visited were always frank and helpful.' His conclusion that a casino was a 'no go zone' and the inherent social concerns of a Labor premier about the possible social impact of such an establishment meant that the first attempt at getting a casino up in Victoria failed.

What is a casino

A chapter of Connor's first exploration into the issue was devoted to explaining what a casino is and how they tend to operate. The basis for this defining of the kind of establishment Connor was ultimately going to encourage the Victorian government to avoid like a plague was the give Victorians who have 'probably never been in a casino' a description of how one operates. His dilemma in grappling with the multiple issues at that time was there was no generic form of a casino. They varied in size, location, and also whether there were more than on casino in a particular location. 'A visitor to a better-class casino could expect to see the gambling area well carpeted with good quality curtains,' Connor observed. 'Security staff employed by the casino will generally be at or near the entrance to check the dress and behaviour of those seeking to enter.' Connor noted that gambling areas would have various tables and games would be played in clusters across a particular room. 'Many casinos, in addition to table games, have one or more keno games and also slot machines.' Those games, Connor said, were typically not far from the gaming tables. The games that were played in the four Australian legal casinos that were operating during the period of the first inquiry included roulette, blackjack, baccarat, mini-dice, two-up, and keno. Tasmania had craps in its list of games permitted on the gaming floor while the casinos in the Northern Territory had slot or poker machines. 'Many other games are played in other casinos around the world but these are the games most likely to be considered for any casino introduced into Victoria,' Connor observed.

The morality of gambling

Could gambling conceivably be banned simply on the basis of it being immoral and causing harm in society? Connor asked the question in his report and delved into morality in an early chapter of his saunter through the gambling landscape, but he was asking that question in the context of Australia already having four legal casinos in operation. Submissions came from various groups including churches. Any answer on a Victorian casino would be provided in an environment where other states had walked down the path of immorality if indeed gambling could be characterised as such. Views on the matter varied between those that offered that two cents worth on the matter. Various clergy from different churches put forward their views on their perspective of gambling with an Anglican cleric by the name of Reverend A D Dargaville who said that there would be a range of opinions in each church about what was considered gambling and what a particular church might discourage its flock from doing. Dargaville, the report said, 'could not recall any statement of any member church of the Victorian Council of Churches which said that gambling per se is wrong'. Another minister, Reverend F B Alcorn, from the Churches of Christ said the belief within his church was that gambling was opposed to the teachings of Christ because 'the warnings of Our Lord with regard to covetousness which seems to be at the very basis of gambling'. Alcorn's take was that greed was not good and that gambling was a manifestation of greed, but that gambling was a matter for an individual's conscience. The Roman Catholic Archbishop of Melbourne at the time, Sir Frank Little, made a statement in June 1982 opposing the establishment of a casino but that statement did not deal with any moral aspect of the establishment of a casino in Victoria. It did, however, address the social impacts of casinos and the Archbishop recommended a Jesuit priest, Father Noel Ryan, provide evidence to the inquiry. Ryan presented an entry from the New Catholic Encyclopaedia that outlined how gambling is seen by the church. 'Gambling, therefore, though a luxury, is not considered sinful except when the indulgence in it is inconsistent with duty,' the encyclopaedia's entry on the topic said. 'Thus it can be sinful when a person has no right to risk the money he bets, either because it is not his own, or because he needs it for the support of his family or for the discharge of other obligations.' The text of the encyclopaedia entry also defines sinfulness in the context of gambling to include the times when a person is gambling with somebody who they know who ought not to be risking their money. Excessive indulgence in gambling is regarded as sinful 'especially when it is market by passionate infatuation'. Ryan also pointed to a source, Bernard Haring's 'The Law of Christ', that he said provided evidence of a difference between Catholic and Protestant views on gambling.

A Mr Mylne appeared for the Melbourne Tourism Authority took what was a predictable route during evidence before the casino inquiry by branding some of the Protestant witnesses appearing before the inquiry as 'wowsers who were afflicted with emotional rigidity and killjoy attitudes', the first Connor report said. It was the one time, Connor observed, that the word 'wowser' had cropped up in the inquiry. 'I reject that submission quite firmly. I consider that, without exception, the Protestant witnesses are thoughtful, caring, unselfish people with high ideals who put their views to me with great sincerity,' Connor observed. He further said that he could not resist thinking that if all members of society were of a similar nature that 'our social ills would be considerably less'. His report acknowledged that those from religious cohorts were arguing a case from social and economic grounds rather than necessarily being dependent on some kind of religious imprimatur that gambling was sinful. Connor did not believe gambling itself was evil and that gambling of various kinds such as betting on the horses and lotteries was already taking place. Gambling activities were helping society via taxes and tax collected made up 11 per cent of Victoria's tax revenue during the 1981–82 financial year.

Influences of crime in casinos

The first Connor report took a deep dive into the risks and benefits of a casino from a community perspective. It was acknowledged in that review and in the many that have taken place since 1983 that gambling in a casino environment would provide an entertaining and legal way to enjoy games of chance. Evidence was tendered during the inquiry that argued that the social benefit of entertainment at a casino-style venue was a factor in favour of establishing a casino. These advantages that have been explored in countless reports on gambling and its social impacts were tempered by Connor's analysis of the kinds of organised crime involvements that could find their way into casino operations. Organised crime had a history of involvement in casinos around the world and for Connor this was to become one of the key concerns throughout his inquiry. The reason for this is that casinos provided a great source of cash, support services can be infiltrated or taken over, networks within the entertainment sector become open, money can be laundered quickly. One of the reasons for casinos being magnets for crooked types is illustrated with an anecdote from a casino in London inspected by Connor and counsel traveling with him. 'In one casino in London which Counsel and I inspected, we were credibly informed that the drop over a period of about an hour was more than 1.75 million pounds and that this was by no means unusual,' Connor said. 'This may serve to illustrate why organised criminals show such an avid interest in legal casinos and why casino operators and government agencies need to wage a never-ending battle to try to keep them out.' Connor was assured by witnesses in favour of establishing a casino in Victoria that the police force would be in a good position to keep organised crime out in an open casino if one was established. Connor's response was incredulous given that the kind of model being spoken about was not operating anywhere in the world that he had looked at.

'In my view that approach simply flies in the face of the wisdom of the world and I can characterise it only as boldness without judgement to assume cheerfully that Victoria can do something which no other country has ever been prepared to do,' Connor said. 'If New Jersey is having trouble keeping organised crime out of casinos which was all concentrated in the tiny island of Atlantic City, how will Melbourne fare with a network of casinos?'

Connor's first verdict

The respected jurist delivered a verdict at that stage that was not going to please any advocate for a casino in Victoria given the series of conclusions he had reached in his extensive sojourn into every perceived benefit, dilemma, and foible that could result from a casino being established. He found that the casinos operating at the time in Tasmania and the Northern Territory were small, well-operated and controlled. Those casinos existed succeeded in environments that were different from Victoria, Connor asserted, and as such the assumption that what works well in Tasmania and the Northern Territory would work similarly in Victoria was flawed. He noted that gambling in Victoria was increasing in popularity and volume and competition between modes of gambling existed. This competition for gambling, however, did not mean that there was a large number of Victorians clamouring to dash into a casino and play roulette and the various other games that such venues provide. 'There is a genuine unstimulated but modest demand by an indeterminate but smallish number of Victorians for casino gambling,' is the description Connor gave to the demand for casinos as he saw it at that stage. Connor also acknowledged in his findings and recommendations that had casinos been established at that time the gambling enterprises would have pocketed about $117 million and the Victorian government would have been able to levy at tax on that golden haul.

His findings noted that there were at least four purposes for which a casino or casinos could be established in Victoria. These reasons were the generation of maximum revenue, the promotion of tourism in resort areas, satiating an unstimulated demand for casino gambling, and having a casino in a large entertainment complex with an operator also being responsible for establishing a convention centre. The convention scenario did not receive a rave review from Connor. 'If a 4,000 delegate convention centre were to be established in Melbourne it would not be financially viable,' Connor said. 'A casino is one way in which it could be financially supported. However, the evidence shows that Melbourne does not need a convention centre for more than 2,500 delegates, which would probably be financially viable without casino support or nearly so.' Connor said that a single entertainment or convention casino would be expected to haul in $78 million of additional economic output for Victoria and provide 2,200 jobs with the figure for any other type of casino that might be established being lower. There was an estimate of the tax a government might expect to derive from the establishment of a casino. Connor suggested that the Victorian government would find itself with $29.5 million in the kitty if a 25% casino tax was levied on the golden lode of $117 million mentioned earlier. Governance and regulation of casinos played a major part in the analysis with Connor concluding the rather obvious: any casinos established need to be controlled by governments closely. There was something else that Connor said governments should distance themselves from where casinos were concerned—it would be impracticable for a government to create or establish 'all but one type of casino and undesirable for it to operate any type of casino'.

Connor's recommendations across all of the casino types he had reviewed were consistent. He played the part of 'Doctor No' with great aplomb. Maximum revenue casinos were out, he said, and the same fate should befall the idea of a casino in a convention centre. What about a resort casino? Connor's response to that suggestion was the equivalent of 'not on your nelly'. The reasons? A casino of any size or flavour would stimulate casino gambling to an unacceptable level, Connor said, and in the next breath there was apparently 'no substantial demand for it'. Any casino would be at risk of becoming the playground of organised crime players as well as possibly attracting street crime. Connor also cast doubts about the ability of casinos to be an effective way to hoover up tax dollars into state coffers. 'I think these considerations outweigh any benefits such as increased economic activity, increased tourism, increased State revenue and social enjoyment,' Connor asserted.

Unobtrusive casinos—casinos that were kind of smallish and not likely to cause too much of a fuss—were briefly entertained by Connor. 'As to an unobtrusive casino I consider that it would not stimulate casino gambling to any appreciable extent, there is a demand for such a casino, here is a good prospect that organised crime and street crime would not be associated with it,' Connor said. It was noted that gamblers in Victoria would have had to go from that state to Tasmania or the Northern Territory to gamble in a casino and that those individuals had a right to highlight the fact that other forms of gambling were catered for in the state but not the type for which they were keen. Unobtrusive casinos could not get past the finnicky legal mind behind the inquiry. Connor cited the introduction of both Tattersalls in the 1950s by the then Premier John Cain Senior and the Totalizator Agency Board in 1959 by Henry Bolte. Cain sought to try and prevent money from leaving the state by establishing a regulated lottery system while Bolte wanted to kill off illegal bookmaking as much as possible. Those two forms of gambling grew exponentially over time, and this is what guided Connor's attitude to even the establishment of a small-scale casino. 'I am not prepared to take the responsibility of recommending even an unobtrusive casino, even though I think it could be introduced initially in a satisfactory form,' Connor said. 'It is admittedly a "think end of the wedge" argument; and such arguments are not always soundly based. This one however is not plucked out of the air, and I believe it is necessary to fly in the face of Victorian history in order to reject it.'

Then there was the small matter of establishing an appropriate regulatory regime that would keep those running venues with casino operations on an appropriately short leash. Connor said that there was no dispute from parties that appeared before his inquiry that the establishment and operations of the casinos should only occur under the most vigilant sets of eyes. 'The broad object of such control is to ensure that casinos are properly run,' Connor said. 'One indispensable requirement for a properly run casino is a proprietor of integrity and ability. Any legislation must provide for adequate machinery for selection of such a proprietor.' A system of government control envisaged by Connor would be staffed by 'honest and capable people' because there is a need for 'competent ongoing strict, even draconian, control becomes clear'. Controls would vary depending on the type of casino but there would be similar internal and other controls that would apply to each casino establishment. 'Control may be infective because it is corrupt, if may also be ineffective because it is incompetent, albeit honest,' Connor observed.

The government led by John Cain put the establishment of any kind of casino on ice when it received the report. The Premier himself believe that poker machines would be detrimental because people would be encouraged to gamble beyond what they could afford and that the machines exploited the working man and woman. This did not mean that the Premier's conservative sentiments on the establishment of casinos were always popular or agreed with by some of his Labor colleagues. The Canberra Times reported on 6 October 1982 that the Minister for Economic Development, Bill Landeryou, took issue with Connor's emerging perspective on casinos. Landeryou told a meeting of the Melbourne Tourism Authority that he saw Connor being difficult on the issue of casinos, but that he hoped that a convention centre would be built with a casino license. He had to personally explain what his comments meant to Cain and withdraw them. Landeryou said he was concerned that there was a media representative in the audience and that a throwaway remark was reported out of context. This was an illustration of what were at least hopes within the ministerial ranks led by Cain that there was a chance for a casino to be built and modernise the state's gambling culture. It was not to be and serious change would need to take place before it would be considered again. That time would come in almost a decade.

Connor resurrected

The Cain government saw itself spiralling into economic difficulties during the latter part of the 1980s and Cain himself resigned in 1990. Various financial scandals such as the collapse of the Pyramid Building Society and the Victorian Economic Development Corporation dogged Cain. His resignation was a circuit breaker, and the elevation of the new premier, Joan Kirner, brought the issue of a casino back on the table because the government needed to find more ways of getting money into state coffers. This meant that Kirner and her colleagues had to find a way of making the idea of a casino fly given the fact that there was a

Connor's second coming was meant to design a regulatory structure for casinos that would ensure a casino or similar venue would be operated and regulated stringently given that the Kirner administration wanted to legalise casinos and electronic gaming machines rather than whether to have a casino in the first place. What changed over almost a decade for Kirner and her colleagues to part with history? The economy needed an injection of revenue and the government needed more tax dollars in the kitty. Getting a casino and other venues using electronic gaming machines would result in revenue gain. Gambling tourism would be minimised because Victorians that would hop over the border into New South Wales or Tasmania would have their own gambling facilities in Victoria. The views within the community regarding casinos had softened to the point where a government entertaining the introduction of both electronic gaming machines and gambling venues could begin to entertain that prospect.

Queensland had a Casino Control Act that was made law in 1983 that Connor thought was a good model for Victoria to emulate in large part. That Queensland law did have one matter to which Connor expressed an exception. Ministers were able to make the decisions related to gambling on the basis of ministerial discretion and Connor wanted to see an independent body in control of that regulation. Connor was still uncomfortable with casinos being established in Victoria as he retained concerns about the way in which the organised crime can weasel its way into a gambling establishment. His second report ended up being the basis of two pieces of legislation that would regulate electronic gaming machines and casinos. The then Minister for Manufacturing and Industry Development, David White, said Melbourne was a city in which all Victorians could take pride and that it should have a 'world-class casino' and that it was also big enough to support and 'unobtrusive club casino'. Victoria's government was working with the New South Wales government on similar casino control issues at that point in time. Both governments were crafting similar laws to regulate the sector based on the second Connor report. 'This consistency of approach will be of benefit to prospective tenderers for casino licences and will offer to both States the same high level of stringent control and regulation of casino operations,' White told the state's parliament on 4 June 1991. The state opposition at the time supported the notion of getting a casino established with an opposition spokesperson in the state's upper house, James Guest, outlining the opposition's support for the notion of a casino. Guest noted that there were concerns from eminent jurists about the capacity of organised crime to use casinos as venues for making money but he said that the economic benefits from casinos were much greater than the risks presented by organised crime. Guest was also careful to ensure that his speech contained a reminder to legislators that would come after him to keep their eyes wide open. 'I wish to start not only with the emphasis that the opposition puts on the responsible regulation of casinos but also with a short description of the fears that have been expressed about casinos because if anyone in years to come reads the debates in Hansard it is important he or she recognises there is a continuing role for members of Parliament to be ever vigilant,' Guest said.

It does not mean that the political opposition would miss an opportunity to deliver a partisan whack around the ears to the Kirner government with Guest using that very same speech to riff on the fact that a Labor government in New South Wales at the time was in a bit of strife over its own granting and administration of gaming or gambling licenses. 'It is now apparent that in New South Wales the actions of a dying Labor government caused its successor to have to pay $30 million to the Hooker Harrah organisation which was found on investigation to be an unsuitable applicant for running a casino anywhere,' Guest said. 'We do not think, as Mr Connor did not think, that the establishment of a casino in Victoria can be done safely if it is done quickly.'

Morphing the regulator over time

The regulatory regime changed over time to accommodate the collective wisdom or otherwise of the governments that were in office in Victoria. The changes in the way the gambling sector was regulated reflected the different views that related to specific casino regulation or regulation of gambling enterprises collectively under one body. This is somewhat like the old story about consultants recommending centralised authority and then switch to decentralised structures and then back to centralised governance when something goes wrong. Regulation of the casino and gambling sector in Victoria followed a similar pattern as politicians and regulators attempt to find a solution to a suite of problems that arise from what society deems to be deviant conduct or behaviour that is not within the social norms expected by the community.

The initial form of casino regulation was as recommended by Connor in his 1991 report. The Victorian Casino Control Authority was established to be an independent regulator for casinos and another regulator called the Victorian Gaming Commission, which was established under the Gaming Machine Control Act, did the same for gaming machines. These two bodies ended up being merged once the control authority for casinos was done with assessing the applicants for the casino licenses following a review of the casino and gaming legislation by the Kennett government that was elected in 1992. That review of the gaming machine laws and effectiveness of regulation took place in September 1993 wound up recommending a merger of the two authorities along with having just one minister responsible for everything to do with gambling. The Victorian Casino Control Authority and the Victorian Gaming Commission became the Victorian Casino and Gaming Authority. It was argued at that time that the merger of the two bodies was a logical step because it would provide consistent regulation of everything to do with gambling as well as establish an office called the Director of Gaming and Betting that had responsibility for the investigation of compliance with laws to do with gambling.

The life cycle of that idea was about a decade because in 2002 it was decided by the then Victorian government that a review into gambling regulation needed to take place. The Finkelstein reports characterises the review that takes place as finding that gambling regulation in Victoria was confusing with responsibilities spread across many pieces of legislation and regulators. Streamlining was recommended, a Victorian Commission for Gambling Regulation was created, and the positions previously in existence called the Director of Gambling and Director of Casino Surveillance were replaced by the new structure. This change came into effect in 2004 with the Gambling Regulation Act bring eight pieces of legislation relevant to the gambling sector into one piece of legislation. The only pieces of legislation left to stand alone were the casino-specific laws: the Casino Control Act and the Management Agreement Act.

Yet another change in regulation hit in 2012 because the government at the time thought it was a reform to shove everything to do with gambling and liquor regulation under one regulatory tent. The legislative DYMO labeller came out again and the Victorian Commission for Gambling and Liquor Regulation was born. It is important to remember that this regulatory evolution broadened the scope of the role of the new gambling sector's regulator from the narrow focus had by the Victorian Casino Control Authority. Three objectives were specified for the casino regulator back when laws were first past in 1991 that related to ensuring casinos were operated free of criminal influence and exploitation, operating a casino in a manner that encourage honest gaming conduct, and promoting tourism and the related economic and employment benefits of such establishments. The regulator morphed in 2012 into a body that need to juggle more than a few balls because of its coverage of all of the matters related to gambling and liquor licences. An interesting point to note is that each regulator up until the 2012 incarnation had independent decision-making powers from the government. The Victorian Commission of Gambling and Liquor Regulation needed to have regard for policy making directions set by the responsible minister. This was not a power intended to instruct the body on how it should resolve regulatory matters. The combined gambling and liquor regulator was also obliged to make sure government policy in the area was put into play. Did this create a real or perceived independence issue for that iteration of regulator? The answer would have to be given in the affirmative.

A case for more change?

A report from the Victorian Auditor-General into the Victorian Commission of Gambling and Liquor Regulation published in February 2017 savaged aspects of the combined regulatory regime. The performance audit found weaknesses in the approach taken to licensing reviews. 'Much work remains and weaknesses in VCGLR's approach mean it still cannot demonstrate that it properly examines and assesses all licensing applications in line with legislative provisions before approving them,' the auditors looking at the regulator found. 'These weaknesses are more significant for liquor applications and arise because VCGLR largely accepts the information provided to it by these applicants at face value.' There was a great reliance, the audit report said, on the part of the regulator on the Victoria Police and the honesty of applicants. It said that there was a need to institute a better risk-based approach to reviewing applications. The same was also noted in the context of compliance inspections. The commission's inspectors were focusing at that time on meeting a number of inspections rather than looking at areas where failure to comply with laws and regulations would lead to a high risk or possibility of harm. 'This approach to compliance does not support the legislative objectives for harm minimisation,' the audit office said.

There is a similar unflattering view presented in the fairly dry and precise language of audit when it came to assessing casino supervision. The regulator was called out by the audit office for failing to appropriately focus on regulating the casino. It had been rotating compliance inspection teams through the casino, but this did not mean that the teams had received every single bit of assistance when it came to guidance, training and management oversight to be able to do its work properly. The problem of inconsistent management oversight had been an issue during 2013 and 2014 with four different people in that particular role within the regulator. 'This further undermined consistency and led to a number of false starts in reviewing and improving the approach to and conduct of compliance inspection activities,' the auditor general's report observed. 'The current manager of casino inspection activities has been in place since October 2014 but is not assigned to the casino on a full-time basis.'

A follow up audit two years later showed that the gambling and liquor regulator had been walking the path towards fixing its processes. The audit team kicking the regulator's tyres on this occasion found that the regulator had established a dedicated team to inspect the casino that has one manager, one team leader, and 12 inspectors with the team located at the casino 24 hours a day to monitor casino affairs. A big green tick was given to the regulator for having adopted a more risk-based approached and bumping up the skill set of staff they have on the job. Formal and informal training was introduced. This included mentoring of staff and the inspection team was also considering training courses on gaming regulation developed in Las Vegas. Further improvements recommended in the audit included a better definition of key risks that relate to the way a casino operates and ensuring regulatory work is linked to mitigation of those risks. In other words: what gets measured gets done. There was also the proposal for a single guide to gambling regulation so that all of the relevant regulators and their responsibilities were outlined in one publication for staff and relevant stakeholders. The fact that the audit office needed to suggest that a publication be created to ensure people involved in such a sensitive and critical task and keeping the gambling sector and a city's single casino under adequate supervision remains puzzling even several years on.

Regulator returns full circle

It would now be obvious from this thumbnail sketch that almost every decade brings a change in regulation to the gambling sector. The gambling and liquor regulation gig was designated a bin fire by the state government in August 2021 and it created yet another regulation to just focus on casino and gambling operations with a division that was dedicated to taking a deep dive into casino regulation. Premier Daniel Andrews told the Victorian community that his government would create a new regulator for casinos and gambling. 'Prior to changes under the Liberal Government in 2012, liquor and gambling were regulated by two standalone control agencies. Our changes will see governance return to a model that has a specific and separate focus on liquor and gambling regulation,' Andrews said. How long the separation of liquor and gambling functions lasts this time around is anybody's guess but the lesson from history is that someone, someplace might well choose to revisit the structure of regulation in order to demonstrate activity.

FROM WILLIAMS TO PACKER—THEN BLACKSTONE?

It was spectacular when it first opened with gas flames and a stellar cast of pop stars and dignitaries, but the casino, hotel and entertainment complex that sits beside the Yarra River at Southbank in Melbourne was not necessarily a part of the government's vision.

The Kirner Government initially wanted a casino to be located at the Docklands. Developing the Docklands was a focus for the Kirner Labor government at the time and a casino that both the state's government and opposition wanted to establish was thought to be an ideal centrepiece for that particular part of the city. The Victorian Minister for Gaming, David White, told the Legislative Council when delivering a second reading speech on the Docklands Authority Bill that the objective was to redevelop the Docklands with a casino as a centrepiece. 'Much of the Docklands is, of course, currently used for port purposes. The government is committed to the continued development of the Port of Melbourne as an efficient commercial port serving the needs of its users and the broader community,' White told parliament in April 1991. He said that the redevelopment strategy would result in those parts of the Docklands being used for port purposes being set aside for new developments. The work in reshaping the Docklands at that time was envisaged to be a private sector initiative with the cooperation of the public sector. A new authority was deemed necessary because government departments and other agencies were not able to undertake the work involved under laws as they existed at the time and that it was best to avoid distracting departments from doing their normal work.

Freshening up the Docklands with a casino and commercial and residential developments was one idea that the besieged Kirner government had in its bag as an initiative to both improve that part of the city. The Liberal and National parties had the smell of Labor's political blood in their nostrils but the Docklands bill was not one where the coalition parties would go into full attack mode. The coalition parties agreed with the overall philosophy of getting the Docklands redeveloped and buzzing. 'The coalition believes the development of the whole Docklands area should be designed to emphasise the spectacular relationship with the water and to create view corridors back to the existing Melbourne skyline,' Mark Birrell, the leader of the opposition in the upper house, said.

The debate was robust despite the fact that the government and the opposition shared the objective to get a casino running in the state of Victoria. The tension in parliamentary debate was around what the opposition considered to be a myopic focus on the part of the government to get a casino in the Docklands. Different kinds of venues were suggested in speeches to parliament and the possible location for a casino was the topic of garden variety political jousting. History records that neither major political party was opposed to having a casino and that it would eventually turn up on the banks of the Yarra as one of the key landmarks for locals and tourists.

Enter Lloyd Williams

Property developer and racing enthusiast Lloyd Williams was at the centre of the successful consortium that put its hand up to take on the mammoth task of building and starting Victoria's first casino. Williams and other prominent figures in the business community such as Ron Walker created what was then known as the Hudson Conway Consortium that was led by the listed company Hudson Conway Limited. Federal Hotels Limited and Carlton and United Breweries were also a part of the consortium. Expressions of interest were called in the latter part of 1991 by the Kirner Government with interest being expressed by a range of domestic and international parties, but the final awarding of a license did not happen at all quickly. Due diligence was conducted into the Hudson Conway bid and a license granted on 19 November 1993. The Kirner government might have kicked that process off in 1991 but it was under the Coalition administration of Jeff Kennett that the casino license was awarded for 40 years.

It was not long after the casino license had been given to the crew behind the Hudson Conway bid that Crown Melbourne ended up being listed on the Australian Stock Exchange. The listing occurred on 9 March 1994 and Crown's equivalent of a casino mini-me that became known as the Galleria Casino opened on 30 June 1994. It was open to run while the larger venue that would be the focus for gambling, entertainment, and dining was being built. The smaller venue, which also allowed training in the casino business, was within walking distance to the site intended for the more spectacular, palatial premises that would begin operating from 8 May 1997. It is interesting to note that this period of Crown's history was only referred to in the royal commission headed by Finkelstein in Victoria. The New South Wales inquiry and the Western Australian Royal Commission were focused exclusively on the Crown companies under the influence of the Packers and specifically on those cultural and systemic issues that rendered the gambling behemoth unsuitable to hold a license. It was the Packer stewardship through its various permutations that caught the eye of the chief inquisitors of every inquiry that looked at this era over the past few years.

Packers enter the play

The larger casino that was a part of the Williams-led regime would run for about two more years before the Packer family entered into the gambling fray with a rather complex takeover tango taking place. Publishing and Broadcasting Limited was the Packer vehicle that hoovered up Crown Melbourne, but that took place in several steps. It might be a cliché but you can only eat an elephant one bite at a time. A merger between Crown and Publishing and Broadcasting Limited took place in June 1999. The Packer play put one Publishing and Broadcasting Limited share on the table for 11 Crown shares. Regulatory and shareholder approvals came through with the merger on 30 June 1999. A couple of other schemes of arrangement needed to be finalised because shareholders in Hudson Conway Limited needed to be given due consideration. Hudson Conway shareholders got two Publishing and Broadcasting shares for three of the Hudson Conway stock. What did this ultimately do? Crown Melbourne became an unlisted and wholly owned subsidiary of the Packer company.

One casino was not going to be good enough for the Packer clan, so it was a case of going West and buying up the shares in something called Burswood Limited. That entity was the holding company of a private company called Burswood Nominees. The Burswood Nominees held the piece of paper that would allow the Packer family access to the opportunity to print money at another casino on the other side of the country. Burswood became Packer territory in September 2004. A bit of thinking went on in the Packer headquarters. They decided that once these two casino licenses were acquired, they would bifurcate the gambling or gaming side of Publishing and Broadcasting Limited from the media business. That split resulted in a couple of listed companies known as Consolidated Media Holdings and Crown Resorts. Media assets were hived off into Consolidated Media Holdings while the gambling licenses that were acquired with the gaming businesses since 1999 lived in Crown Resorts. Crown Resorts was listed on 3 December 2007 on the Australian Securities Exchange.

'The move to a pure play gaming enterprise has allowed Crown to focus on developing its business strategy which is underpinned by high cash generating businesses in Australia, a conservative financial structure and increasing geographical diversification,' James Packer, then executive chairman of Crown, said in the 2008 annual report for the listed gambling giant. Packer was able to announce a $370.1 million profit that year. The money printing machine would report eyewatering profits as well as worrying losses over much of the next decade.

The 2008 annual report also provides an illustration of the various other venues Crown had accumulated an interest in. This was not just a business that was solely playing on Australian territory. Packer's report to shareholders spoke about the proposed acquisition of 100 per cent of the Cannery Casino Resorts in the United States while interests that Crown had in Macau through Melco Crown Entertainment Limited were said to have been trading well in the first full year. Crown Resorts held a 37.9 interest in the Macau gambling outfit. Canada had also got itself a Crown presence at that time with a Crown-Macquarie Bank joint venture called New World Gaming. Crown and Macquarie went fifty-fifty to buy the Gateway casino operator. Crown had a 50 per cent interest in Betfair, a betting exchange that operated across Australia and New Zealand, as well as a 50 per cent interest in Aspinalls, which is an entity that operated four casinos in the United Kingdom at that time. The Crown business was one that had its tentacles in various gambling and gaming markets and that appetite was unlikely to be satiated over time.

It was operations in Macau in particular, and the entanglement with individuals that had associates involved in criminal activity, that ended with a deep dive into Crown's operations, the nature of junkets, and the legal pursuit of Crown staff—that resulted in custodial sentences for people that were working in China to attract new business to Crown. Questions about operations in Macau and the other issues above would eventually lead to three declarations of Crown being suitable to hold a license.

The Melco transaction and the controversy

Packer and Laurence Ho began a joint venture in 2006 called Melco Crown. The creation of this particular joint venture saw Stanley Ho, Laurence's father, give his boy control over the Macau-based casino empire. The senior Ho was linked over the years with organised crime and money laundering and there was a ban on him having any involvement in a casino enterprise in Sydney. There was also a condition imposed on Crown that required it to ensure that Stanley Ho or any entities that were in some way related to him from buying a direct, indirect or beneficial interest in a Crown venue in Sydney. There were 58 entities in an undertaking signed by Crown that had some kind of link to Stanley Ho. Any involvement with these associated entities could be perceived as Crown breaching an undertaking.

Great Respect was one of those entities that controlled a trust for the Ho family. It had a large share in Melco International that wanted to buy into Crown and was a Stanley Ho associate that was specifically banned from having an involvement. Why did this impact on transactions that Melco international wanted to do with Crown? Stanley Ho was a beneficiary of Great Respect. Great Respect owned a slab of shares Melco International and Melco wanted to buy into Crown. This meant that any transaction consummated between Crown and Melco would attract the attention of vigilant regulators. The Bergin report declared that there was no breach of the Barangaroo restricted license or any other regulatory agreement.

Private equity sticks its head up

The three inquiries into Crown would bring an inevitable vulture or three circling around what was perceived to be a carcass ready to be picked apart. Private equity concern Blackstone bobbed up in March 2021 offering to buy an organisation that had just had its nose bloodied and reputation well and truly gored by a report submitted to a government agency focusing on its culture, competence, and compliance. This was not Blackstone's first entry into getting its paws on Crown shares given that it already owned a stake in the gambling business when it bought 10 per cent of Crown from Melco Resorts in April 2020. Those shares were bought from Melco Resorts for $8.15 a share. That purchase added to a portfolio of activity in the gambling sector that Blackstone has already established. Blackstone's approach to Crown on 22 March 2021 was an attempt to acquire all of the shares in the gambling and entertainment giant. There was an initial price—an ambit claim, if you will—of $11.85 cash per share. It wasn't long, however, before the Crown board of directors received a modification to the initial proposal in a section related to regulatory approval conditions. This was a period where Blackstone was hitting Crown with proposals and amendments in quick succession. Yet another communication from Blackstone lobbed onto the desk of the Crown board of directors on 10 May 2021. Blackstone had given them another proposal with an acquisition price of $12.35 per share. Crown's board of directors told Blackstone to get nicked.

Blackstone kept trying to ask Crown out to the dance and sent another proposal to Crown's board asking for their offer of $12.50 a share on 19 November 2021. The proposal was evaluated by the Crown board of directors. 'The Crown Board is of the view that the Proposal does not represent compelling value for Crown shareholders,' the board of directors said in a market release issued on 2 December 2021.

'However, the Crown Board has offered Blackstone the opportunity to access non-public information to allow Blackstone to undertake initial due diligence inquiries on a non-exclusive basis so that it can formulate a revised proposal that adequately reflects the value of Crown.' The private equity pundits got their hands on non-public information to have another crack at successfully courting the Crown board and the board of the gambling giant took to the market with an announcement to tell them there was something that looked viable that had hit the table. This revised proposal—that lifted the acquisition price from $12.50 per share as submitted by Blackstone in November 2021 to $13.10 per share—was described by the Crown board in more favourable terms on 13 January 2022. 'Should Blackstone make a binding offer at a price of no less than $13.10 cash per share then, subject to the parties entering into a binding Implementation Agreement on terms and conditions acceptable to Crown, it is the Crown Board's current unanimous intention to recommend that shareholders vote in favour of the proposal in the absence of a superior proposal and subject to an Independent Expert concluding (and continuing to conclude) that the proposed transaction is in the best interests of Crown shareholders.'

The deal done?

Crown's negotiations with Blackstone culminated with a market release that put the future of the gambling giant in no doubt. The private equity company had put forward an offer that Crown's board said was attractive for shareholders and it recommended that the shareholders vote in favour of the Blackstone proposal. A scheme of arrangement would give Crown shareholders $13.10 per share and that amount—referred to as the scheme consideration—is based on the share price as at 18 November 2021 of $9.90. This share price was the last struck on the exchange before Blackstone put forward a proposal for acquisition. The initial offer from Blackstone was $12.50 per share. Crown's equity is valued in the scheme consideration at an eyewatering $8.9 billion and that figure is $845 million more that the price offered by the private equity play in March 2021 while Crown was still feeling the welts from the Bergin review at a time when Finkelstein was warming up for his deep dive into Crown affairs.

The Blackstone offer had various conditions attached to it. These conditions are that an independent expert will need to issue a report that determines the proposed scheme is in the interest of shareholders, the Foreign Investment Review Board needs to give Blackstone's acquisition a big green tick, every gaming regulatory authority needs to give their own version of approval, no gaming regulatory even or material adverse change occurs, and other 'customary conditions'. Blackstone lodged various applications with relevant bodies for approval and there were other issues that the company itself sought to highlight to the market. 'The Implementation Deed is subject to customary deal protections for Blackstone including no shop, no talk and no due diligence obligations on Crown. Crown is also bound by other customary provisions including notification obligations and matching rights in the event of a competing proposal,' Crown's market release observed.

Chairman Switkowski told the market that the board backed the proposal going ahead provided all of the conditions related to regulatory approvals were met and the independent expert agreed that the offer from Blackstone is suitable to proceed. 'When considering any proposal, the Crown Board has consistently stated it is committed to maximising value for Crown shareholders,' Switkowski said. 'The Crown Board and management have made good progress in addressing a number of significant challenges and issues emerging from the COVID-19 pandemic and various regulatory processes.'

Switkowski also told the market that uncertainty remained about several factors and that the all-cash offer from Blackstone gave shareholders certainty of value. The chairman said the offer from Blackstone was better than the one the private equity play put on the table in March 2021 and it should be considered as an offer worthy of shareholder consideration.

Crown's McCann echoed Switkowski's sentiments and reinforced that the offer was compelling. 'The price appropriately reflects the value of Crown's world-class assets and global reputation for premium service and experiences,' McCann said. 'The agreement with Blackstone also highlights the strength of the Crown brand and confidence in our future as we emerge from some challenging times, which is welcome news for our people, customers and stakeholders.' How the Blackstone deal proceeds in the context of the regulatory attention that Crown Resorts has received over the past several years will remain something for the future. What is known, however, is Blackstone is unafraid to invest in gambling and entertainment venues and the private equity play has kept control of properties while the gambling operation may be run by a separate company that has the necessary local expertise to keep an operation relatively clean and compliant with regulations.

PACKER AND THE PULLING OF STRINGS

As previously said, I remain committed to serving the best interests of Crown and, most importantly, you.

Andrew Demetriou, former director of Crown Resorts, to James Packer, April 2019

Ken I think all of you have had your heads in the sand this year. We never meet our plans and I'm sick of it. Make sure for your own sake that we achieve the FY 20 [the 2020 financial year] plan.

James Packer to Kenneth Barton by email on 1 March 2019

The language employed by Mr Packer reflects aggressive expectation and entitlement and properly characterises Mr Packer's communications as instructions, not mere requests for information or the giving of 'advice'.

The Bergin Report, February 2021

The Blackstone acquisition of Crown represents the exit from the main battlefield of business of a family that has been omnipresent ever since Frank and Kerry Packer began their involvement in the ownership of media outlets in Australia. Media reports had the mother lode that James Packer would wind up with following the Blackstone transaction at around an eyewatering $3 billion. The junior Packer's life had been well documented through media accounts of his various health and relationship issues along with his business highlights and lowlights. The corporate titan's influence over Crown and the way in which he exercised it during his time on the board—and once he left—was extraordinary. It was given a lot of real estate in the two main reports published at the time of writing with ample evidence being provided that Packer the younger had enormous influence. That influence was able to be exercised because Packer was able to create a team of directors and mangers that would be loyal, 'committed and steadfast'. These directors were, according to the Finkelstein report, so committed, so loyal and so steadfast that they were people on whom he could depend at any time. Packer would be a constant presence even after he had no formal role as a chair or director on the board of Crown-related companies.

How was Packer a constant influence on Crown affairs? Finkelstein's report noted that Packer used his influence over the various directors and managers, managing to get them to reveal what was going on in the casino business. It was also noted that Packer used his influence over Crown to 'suit his own interests, even after his resignation from Crown and CPH'. The Bergin inquiry saw questioning of Packer related to his influence and power over the organisation. One line of questioning related to there being evidence of managers and board members having a 'desire to please'. Packer told Bergin that it was possible that there was a desire to please him but that he was not necessarily always pleased. Packer, you see, comes across as a rather hard marker when it comes to assessing the work of senior managers and budgets and forecasts were a topic that kept him wanting to keep them on their toes. 'If you look at our financial budgets and forecasts, they never please me because we always missed them, and that was probably right towards the top of my list of important things, so I don't think it would be fair to say that I was always being pleased by people,' Packer told Bergin during his appearance.

Packer explained the manner in which the board oversight of management occurred when he appeared before the Western Australian inquiry looking into whether Crown Perth should continue to have a license to print money. He told counsel assisting the Western Australian examination of the Crown business that the board was kept up to date during board meetings. It was, according to Packer, an 'iterative process' where the board of directors learned whether the management was made of the right stuff and capable of walking their talk. 'Management would put forward budgets, would put forward capital proposals, would put forward things of that nature,' Packer said. 'After a while, after being on the board, you would get a sense of whether the people that were putting forward those arguments were likely to deliver on what they were proposing.' Packer also noted after further questioning about the role of the chairman of the board would also be 'to make sure that the company is in compliance with its regulatory obligations'.

The interesting issue for Packer, however, is that the Perth inquiry niggled him over his expressed 'full confidence' in the chief executive office of Crown Perth, Barry Felstead, but Packer as chairman of the board was not in attendance at boards meetings for several years. Counsel assisting put to Packer that he had left things to management and that he stopped attending boards meetings when he pulled stumps and moved to live overseas in 2013. 'I missed the next four Burswood board meetings, yes,' Packer said. Counsel assisting further prompted Packer. 'Well, you actually missed them for about the next three years, didn't you?' Counsel assisting queried.

Packer admitted he had missed board meetings as the chairman of Crown Perth over almost three years and that it took at least a year for Alexander to become acting chair and then chairman. Packer admitted that he should have attended board meetings of Crown Perth or resigned from the board of Crown Perth if he was unable to fully participate. He did, however, tell the Perth-based inquiry that he attended the board of the parent company and as such was aware and briefed on all of the Perth issues as presented in the information pack prepared by the company. The more extraordinary evidence that unfolded before all three inquiries in various forms was why Packer retained a high level of intimacy with the details of Crowns operations—even details to which he was unentitled—once he left the boards of the entities with which hem his family, and the various Packer companies were associated since 1999.

He resigned—why was he still involved?

It was on 21 March 2018 that Crown advised the world in a pithy 54-word market release that Packer, the Australian corporate titan, had resigned as a director of Crown Resorts. There was no great fanfare from the company other than to state Packer had resigned for personal reasons and for Alexander, who was the executive chairman of Crown at that time, to acknowledge Packer's contribution to the board in one line. 'We have appreciated James' contribution to the Board and respect his decision to step down from his role as a director at this time,' Alexander said. The Bergin report cited a spokesperson that had said that Packer resigned as a director of various entities within the Consolidated Press Holdings Group in order to seek treatment for mental health issues. Resigning from the boards of Crown and Consolidated Press for personal reasons did not mean that Packer would keep away from Crown affairs. The three reports emanating from the inquiries held into Crown noted that Packer remained omnipresent, and this was in part facilitated by a controlling shareholder protocol that was deemed necessary to ensure that Packer got information he required as a person with a large shareholding in the company. This was one way of satiating the demands of the dominant shareholder for information related to Crown.

Critical to any discussion about the protocol is the fact that the controlling shareholder protocol set down a series of guidelines for the directors and managers of Crown so they could determine precisely what kind of information Packer should get and what information ought to be withheld from him given its nature. Bergin's report cites a section within the protocol that require directors and senior managers to consider before passing information on to Packer and Consolidated Press Holdings. This section is known as Section 2.3 in the document and it demanded of people a consideration about whether the disclosure of information met certain criteria. One of the criteria was whether the bests interests of the company would be served by Packer knowing things that he had no genuine need to know. What of the material given to him was something that was nice to know rather than essential for decision making? Board members and managers had to consider whether there was any likely detriment to the company if disclosure was made and whether disclosure would benefit somebody else. It is suggested that improper disclosures ought not to be made and also whether any disclosure that is being considered is in fact a breach of confidence. How did this little gem of a section go in practice? Not particularly well.

It was during evidence given before the Bergin inquiry that the ability of Packer to pull strings even when he had no official responsibility nor right to certain information became clear. The sharing of information with him when he had no official role within the board or executive of the companies was noted in some detail across the two Bergin inquiry tomes. Packer expected people to feed him information, and heaven help the person that did not keep the drip of information—sometimes material to which he was unentitled—going. He would press relentlessly in order to get what he required from specific board members that would feed him company details. A failure of somebody, anybody, of whom a request was made to respond in a timely manner 'for your own sake' to Packer could be met with termination of employment. 'The irresistible conclusion from the evidence is that Mr Packer took the view and behaved in a manner consistent with the view that he was still in control of Crown,' Bergin said. 'He was endorsing cost-cutting measures; he was demanding that financial plans met his requirements; and he was still deciding whether directors should stay in particular positions.' Bergin observed that Packer said it as the job of certain executives to deliver on requests Packer made of them. 'He did not appreciate that his departure from the Crown board did not entitle him to do so,' Bergin noted.

Who told Packer what?

There were people who spoke to Packer about confidential matters concerning Crown using the controlling shareholder protocol as the basis for doing so. Key among them were individuals that were Consolidated Press Holdings' nominees on the Crown board and others that had close links to the Packer family in one form or another. It was noted by the Bergin report, for example, that Michael Johnston, the former Consolidated Press finance director, was on the Crown board from 6 July 2007. He departed roles in both Crown and Consolidated Press on 10 February 2021. The obligations Johnston had to both entities during his time as a director of Crown could, according to Bergin, lead to conflicts of interest.

The Bergin and Finkelstein reports walk a reader through Johnston's multiple roles across both Crown and Consolidated Press. Johnston informed Packer about the VIP working group and also continuing updates on the VIP business. It was Bergin who concluded that Johnston's conflicting role contributed to a worsening of risk management problems and corporate governance issues. 'Mr Packer expected Mr Johnston to inform him of any important issues regarding Crown, particularly in relation to the VIP International business. Mr Johnston showed complete loyalty to Mr Packer,' Bergin said.

The 10 February 2021 also saw another director of Crown and Consolidated Press resign. Guy Jalland—who was known as one of Packer's key advisers within Consolidated Press—was appointed to the board of Crown in June 2018 and he was also the managing director of Consolidated Press at the same time. He also triggered the use of the protocol to pass confidential material on to Packer.

Influencing management

The Bergin report findings also focused on Crown senior managers and their briefing of Packer on a range of matters. John Alexander's role as a director and an executive at Crown—Alexander was both executive deputy chairman of Crown for a couple of years before taking the mantle of executive chairman from February 2017 to January 2020—meant that he exercised the protocol to keep Packer briefed on a range of matters. His loyalty to Packer, according to Bergin, was on all evidence very strong and he supplied Packer with information on a range of issues that included briefings about board meetings and 'in camera' sessions of the board. Packer kept Alexander on his toes with demands for information and evidence before the Bergin inquiry led to the conclusion he had an involvement in decision making at Crown despite having no board or management involvement. Alexander exited the board in October 2020.

Alexander was not the only person that was influenced by Packer. Kenneth Barton was the chief financial officer of Crown for a decade before being appointed the chief executive officer in January 2020. He was a director of Crown Melbourne, a director of the controversial Riverbank and Southbank, and also a director of Crown Resorts. Barton provided daily reports on Crown finances to Packer and this continued when Packer resigned from all of his company officer roles with Crown and Consolidated Press. Packer admitted to instructing Barton to give him specific information and reports. Barton was expected to do what Packer requested. This information was also provided by Barton to maintain what he described as a strong and open relationship with Consolidated Press and Packer himself. Another of Crown's senior management heavyweights, Barry Felstead, was the chief executive officer of Crown Perth from March 2007 to August 2013, and those roles were followed by an appointment to various Crown-related boards on which he remained until 2021. Felstead briefed Packer extensively on issues related to the VIP International business and Felstead communicated extensively with Packer when he exited all of this Crown and Consolidated Press roles. Another executive involved in the VIP International business, Ishan Kunaratnam, was named in the Bergin report as a close Packer family friend and that he was a Packer appointment to be a special adviser to Packer on the international business. Kunaratnam—also known as Ratnam—dealt with international clients, briefed Packer on international business matters, and Bergin found that Packer had significant influence on Kunaratnam's work at Crown.

Directors and the Packer influence

The board of Crown did over the life of Packer's involvement have a parade of characters that were in some way or form linked to the Packer family in different ways. A key director for part of the last decade was Andrew Demetriou, the former chief executive officer of the Australian Football League. Demetriou was approached on two occasions to join the board of Crown Casino by Packer. His first introduction to the Packer family was through the late Kerry Packer, but the son of Kerry tapped him on the shoulder to be a Crown director in 2012. Demetriou refused to entertain board membership. Packer had another crack at asking Demetriou to come and play at Crown with him in 2015. Demetriou had pulled stumps at the AFL the previous year after 11 years as the chief executive officer looking after a football code. Something had clearly changed by January 2015 and Demetriou accepted a position on Crown's board as a non-executive director. He was appointed chairman of Crown in January 2020. Demetriou frequently shared board meeting details and other confidential information with Packer. It was during the Bergin inquiry's public hearings that Demetriou was asked what he thought briefing Packer on board meeting details would do to help Crown's corporate culture. The former AFL chief told counsel assisting at that time he thought he was operating under the protocol, knew he had to be cautious about the kind of information he provided Packer, and that Packer's advice would be of benefit to all shareholders. It was acknowledged by Demetriou that the clause requiring directors and senior managers to think carefully about the material shared with Packer was not followed.

Two other directors were specifically highlighted by the Finkelstein royal commission's report into Crown as having close links to Packer. The doyen of advertising and media buying, Harold Mitchell, was a director of Crown for just on a decade but there was no evidence presented to the Bergin inquiry that pointed to Packer having any influence over Mitchell. Evidence was presented about a significant loan provided by Packer's father, Kerry, to Mitchell to bail him out of financial strife. Mitchell had signed personal guarantees—four of them—for a business that was known as 'The Big Banana'. Packer gave him a $1.9 million to assist with the problems he was facing. Michell told the Bergin inquiry that the amount was given with no strings attached and that he had paid it off. Mitchell told the inquiry that the suggestion the loan would have made him less independent as a director of Crown was not true. Benjamin Brazil, a finance and investment professional who had spent time during his career with Macquarie Bank, was another director that had a close connection with and was a personal friend of Packer. The Bergin report noted that Brazil had the best interests of Crown at heart whenever he considered matters on the board. 'Mr Brazil was taken through a series of emails in which he appeared to be assisting Mr Packer,' the Bergin report said. 'He resisted any suggestion that he might lack independence and referred to examples of speaking stridently against and opposing proposals for which CPH had some enthusiasm.' Bergin concluded that Brazil's self-perception as an individual that would act in the interests of Crown irrespective of any links with Packer was 'accurate and justified'.

What Packer was not told

Emphasis was placed during inquiries on the influence and power that Packer exercised both during his time as one of the people in charge of governance of various Crown entities and under the controlling shareholder protocol established in 2018. It is appropriate that any analysis of Packer's continuous attempts to influence goings on receives scrutiny but Packer—like other board members—has another problem during his time at Crown. There were matters about which Packer was not made aware and these were among the material areas in inquiry across three jurisdictions over two years.

Packer was not told about matters related to the Chinese authorities questioning staff in China despite the fact that he was the chairman of Crown when the Chinese were making their inquiries. It is also clear from evidence that Johnston and Felstead did not tell Packer of the fact a Crown employee was being questioned but this was concealed from the chairman of the company. This was not the only issue that people failed to bring to Packer's attention. Crown management knew the banks were busy trying to clean house when it came to bank accounts that were held by the Southbank and Riverbank subsidiaries of the Melbourne and Perth Casinos following indications that crooks might be using those accounts for the purposes of money laundering. Packer told the Bergin inquiry that he was unaware of these companies that were the conduit through which millions of dollars were funnelled and later pushed through into Crown. It is clear that these were instances in which Packer was blindsided by his own administration. 'Perhaps this was another indication of not providing the "bad news" to Mr Packer. In any event, it is inexplicable that the Chairman of the Company should not have been advised that its major banker had decided to close a subsidiary's account because of the indicia of money laundering,' the Bergin report said. 'It is also clear that Mr Packer was not made aware of similar concerns being entertained by Commonwealth Bank of Australia and ASB Bank Limited with the ultimate closure of both accounts for the same concerns.' It is clear from the various elements of evidence present that management was not keen to share negative developments with the boss, but that also means that the culture of the organisation needed serious attention. How can any chairman and, indeed, any board member take responsibility for matters that management had deliberately or inadvertently concealed from those in charge of governance? Such instances of management failing to brief boards appropriately so they can take appropriate action at the governance level may explain to observers of regulatory activity in Australia why members of prominent company boards receive no action letters from the Australian Securities and Investments Commission in high profile corporate matters.

	Term in Office
Crown Resorts Ltd Directors who resigned during the inquiry processes	
Helen Coonan	2011–2021
Michael Johnston	2007–2021
Guy Jalland	2018–2021
Andrew Demetriou	2015–2021
Kenneth Barton	2020–2021
Harold Mitchell	2011–2021
John Poynton	2018–2021
John Horvath	2010–2021
Antonia Korsanos	2018–2021

Crown Resorts Limited directors appointed during or just after the inquiry processes	
Zygmunt (Ziggy) Switkowski	2021–ongoing
Anne Ward	2022–
Nigel Morrison	2021–
Jane Halton	2018–
Steve McCann	2021–

WASH CYCLE

There is no evidence to support the suggestion that Crown made source of funds enquiries in respect of deposits into the Southbank and Riverbank accounts.

The Bergin Report, February 2021

The fact that there is a large volume of cash transacted in a casino does not mean that it is money laundering. It obviously equates with a very large risk of money laundering.

The Bergin Report, February 2021

Money laundering is a piece of financial crime jargon that simply means the attempt made by people that have stolen funds to mask their origin and make them appear legitimate. There are different ways in which funds can be laundered but the end objective for the crooks, swindlers, scammers, and drug traffickers is to minimise the likelihood of law enforcement, tax authorities, intelligence agencies and other observers being able to trace the origins of the funds. Methods will vary but the objective—to conceal as best as possible the possession of stolen funds—is always the same.

What happens when laundering occurs

Consider the scenario where a bad actor has money acquired as a result of engaging in any kind of criminal act. It does not matter what the act itself might be for the moment. The crook needs to get the funds someplace so that they do not appear to be the proceeds of crime even though they're as guilty as sin. A first step in moving things along is what is known as placement. Placement involves a crook putting funds into a legitimate part of the financial system. They might put funds into bank accounts in dribs and drabs while doing their best to avoid arousing suspicion using what is known as transaction structuring. That does not always work for the person behind the crime as shall be seen below. Placement will then be followed by a separate stage known as layering. This stage will often involve further transactions that could involve many bank accounts or corporate or trust structures that can be used to further disaggregate and disperse the stolen funds. A third stage referred to by financial crime experts is known as integration. Integration will typically involve the reinvestment of the stolen funds in some form and that could be investment in a legitimate business, purchase of property, and the purchase of any kind of physical asset. It should be noted that a crook will not necessarily succeed when they try to to be tricky and attempt to hide stolen funds. The audit trail of transactions would need to be well concealed.

Digitisation and money laundering

Digitisation of financial services has also meant that traditional methods of money laundering can be used along with methods of laundering that were getting traction. Law enforcement and intelligence agencies and regulators are monitoring money laundering activities in order to better understand where the money laundering threats are and who might be doing the digital shuffle of funds to move their illicit proceeds from a well-regulated jurisdiction to one that may be perceived to be more sympathetic to the wishes of colourful characters related to finding a reasonably secure parking spot for their ill-gotten gains. Laundering of funds does not just take place in the context of currency deemed legal tender such as the American or Australian dollar. Bad actors may choose to try and obscure their gains from criminal activity from view by using any of a number of digital so-called currencies or digital assets such as bitcoin or etherium. These digital assets or currencies become a way of converting dollars into a digital asset that can be traded for other things. Curious online vendors that use messaging apps to sell weapons, drugs, and counterfeit currency will often request to be paid in bitcoin or a similar kind of currency because it's harder for law enforcement agencies to trace.

Digitisation of financial services does not mean that cash-based laundering is dead. Casinos are establishments where domestic and international criminal gangs will seek to morph pinched pennies into something that appears to be clean currency. One look at the various services casinos provide to patrons points to a series of possible exposures to money laundering. Casinos keep customer accounts and exchange foreign currencies. Electronic funds transfers are undertaken by casinos and they also both write and cash cheques. A consultancy engaged by Crown Resorts looking at anti-money laundering issues identified 51 ways in which money laundering can take place.

Laundering case studies

Australia's anti-money laundering regulator, The Australian Transactions Reports and Analysis Centre, tracks money laundering and terrorist financing activities in Australia and publishes regular reports, risk assessments and guidance that provide an update on the prevalence of the different types of money laundering. A series of publications setting out typologies and case studies of how money laundering takes place highlight several instances in which casinos were used as one way of trying to hide where cash came from. AUSTRAC's case studies point to examples where suspicious matter reports from casino management assisted in taking shady characters away from casino bars and putting them behind ones in a prison. AUSTRAC's examples provide an illustration of how the system works when casinos, regulators and law enforcement agencies cooperate to get outcomes.

Suspected drug trafficker loses gamble

One example outlined in AUISTRAC's 2014 compendium of money laundering case studies is of a person who was suspected of wanting to launder the proceeds of 'drug related activity' through bank accounts and an account with a casino. The person of interest deliberately planned to launder cash through a bank as well as a gambling venue. Bank staff reported that the five lots of cash totalling $41,500 was deliberately structured to be under the $10,000 threshold that required the bank to report transactions to AUSTRAC and 'smelled of mothballs'. Bank staff lodged five suspicious matter reports anyway because the suspect made the five deposits over a four-day-period into his own bank account.

The suspect then moved $40,000 from a personal bank account into a bank account of an Australian casino. A further $40,000 was plonked directly into the casino account by the suspect. There was also another report by the bank to AUSTRAC when the individual received $131,000 from the casino in his account. That same casino also sent a suspicious matter report to AUSTRAC because the casino had observed that the individual concerned would 'become aggressive when casino staff requested identification as part of the casino's normal identification procedures for customers cashing out gaming chips'. The cashing out of chips was also being done under the $10,000 threshold and it was suggested that this was to avoid the need to provide proof of identity to staff. This conduct wound up giving this individual the ultimate reward of two and a half years imprisonment for attempting to traffic a controlled drug after being sprung with 4.5 kilograms of cannabis by a police dog at an Australian airport.

Crime syndicate gets caught out by casino reports

An organised crime syndicate—with members of an Asian background—that was caught out by AUSTRAC and other authorities for committing fraud had a company they used as a front for a couple of enterprises. The first set up to arrange for the migration of overseas students to Australia, but that company was also a vehicle for a fraud scheme involving credit cards. This credit card scam involved exploiting vulnerable Malaysian nationals with gambling debts to buy goods that were easily resold by using dodgy credit cards. The scheme involved the fraudsters supplying their debt-laden recruits with false identities that enabled them to get bank accounts and apply for loans. The recruits would then be given credit cards and be used as mules by buying goods of high value with credits cards obtained under false identities that the syndicate would resell. Syndicate members would pay the recruits—as AUSTRAC describes them—an amount to pay off their gambling debts.

AUSTRAC and law enforcement bodies found that it was likely the proceeds from this fraudulent credit card scheme were being used to buy property and getting laundered through casinos. One casino's suspicious matter report said that a syndicate member had cashed in $32,000 worth of chips into cash but the individual had supplied a dodgy casino identity card that was not linked to gambling activity at that casino.

'Further investigation by the casino found that the same person had previously supplied a different casino identity card for other transactions on the same day,' AUSTRAC said. 'Significant cash transaction reports submitted to AUSTRAC also linked the syndicate member to four other gaming chip cash-outs totalling AUD $59,000 over a 14-month period. The cash-outs were either conducted on the same day, or in the same week.' Prison sentences were handed to two syndicate members who were found guilty of fraud related charges.

Good behaviour bond for suspect caught gambling

A further case study revealed that AUSTRAC's files helped fill the gaps for an enforcement agency chasing an individual suspected of being a part of an international money laundering operation. This was a story with a twist because it involved investigators identifying three Chinese airline crew that had thought they could sneak out of Australia without declaring $100,000. Two of the adventurous crew members were caught out with a mixture of Australian and foreign currency totalling $30,000 to $40,000 respectively while the third crew member living the life in the fast lane had $30,000 in foreign currency. These three individuals led authorities to folks based in Australia that were involved in cross-border money laundering games.

This particular suspect had a history of gambling at a casino and was the subject of a series of suspicious matter reports. 'The [reports highlighted inconsistent gaming activity at a casino by the suspect. One [report] described how the suspect had lost more than AUD $3 million in one year while gambling in the casino,' AUSTRAC said. 'The suspect's losses in other years were comparatively smaller, ranging from approximately AUD $3,000 to AUD $30,000.'

Authorities tracked the suspect and caught them red handed with a bag containing $200,000 in cash. It was then established that the suspect had been the source of funds that the three airline crew members had been attempting to take overseas.

The international money laundering scheme also involved the suspect liaising with a remittance service provider's employee who had transferred funds on behalf of the money launderer to China. 'An Australian bank submitted [a report] about this individual's activities after she made two unusually large cash deposits totalling AUD $600,000 on the same day to the same bank account,' AUSTRAC explained. 'AUSTRAC also received two significant cash transaction reports for the two large deposits.' It was also alleged by investigators that the same individual kept themselves rather busy at the behest of the suspect. She deposited a further $800,000 on a separate day. This money laundering tale ended with the suspect being charged with dealing with property reasonably suspected of being the proceeds of crime. They should have counted themselves lucky because the sentence was a 12-month good behaviour bond.

These case studies are just a few samples of AUSTRAC's work in which crooks used casinos and other gambling venues to muddy the waters about the origins of their activities. These examples, however, are illustrations in which gambling venues have assisted the authorities by reporting suspicious conduct. AUSTRAC and other agencies are then able to assemble a picture from the various pieces of data of the activities engaged in by a suspect. What happened in the case of money laundering where Crown Resorts' operations were concerned?

Subsidiary bank accounts and laundering practice

Money laundering in various forms did take place through the bank accounts of two subsidiaries associated with the two casino properties that were operated by Crown Resorts. These accounts were critical in the attempt to provide cover and privacy for those individuals that were wanting to digitally shuffle funds into an account with Crown Resorts for the purpose of frittering them away on whatever particular game took their fancy. Millions of dollars went through these accounts each year, but the more curious question is why this was allowed to keep going for so long. Was this a case of Crown never seeing a dollar it didn't like at the peak of this activity?

Privacy for patrons?

The two entities were known as Southbank, which was a subsidiary for the Crown Melbourne operation, and Riverbank, a subsidiary linked to the Burswood casino. Southbank was actually an incorporated shelf company that was established back when the casino first started its operations in 1996 with the incorporated entity having at least one company secretary as required by law. The entity known as Riverbank, however, started life as Burswood Partnership Pty Ltd on the 15 May 2003 but then changed to Riverbank on 14 November 2005. Both of these entities had accounts with global banking juggernaut HSBC. That banking relationship was ended by HSBC when it conducted a review of its gaming sector relationships in 2013. Southbank moved its banking business across to the Commonwealth bank and the managers at Riverbank opened an account with the ANZ.

Account details for both of the subsidiaries were made known to the clients of both casinos with express instructions given to the players to ensure that a patron number, a unique identifier for that gambler, was supplied so that any funds deposited would end up in the right pigeonhole in the casino's finance system. Using an identifier of this nature in transaction details would also mean that a series of deposits structured to avoid the mandatory reporting threshold of $10,000 could be transferred and all of the amounts belonging to one client would wind up in the same place anyway. There were, however, instructions given by Crown to patrons for what to do when the client or patron identification number was not supplied. Crown required some form of evidence of a deposit in order for a deposit to be put into their casino account. 'This could be done by providing the cage or VIP International unit with a receipt from the bank, or from internet banking, or a phone screenshot setting out the nature of the transfer that had occurred,' the Bergin Report observed. 'The reconciliation of the patron number with the deposit was performed by the VIP International unit or the cage.' Periodic transfers would be facilitated by casino finance or credit staff from the Southbank and Riverbank accounts to the accounts of the casino properties themselves.

Inconsistent transaction records

Problems in consistency of record keeping would emerge and the lack of consistency would bamboozle staff responsible for reporting on the casino's compliance with anti-money laundering rules. Amounts that lobbed into the casino accounts would have to be recorded in the customer relationship database called the SYCO database that Crown's properties have for regular customers. The database records the basic details of a customer that include the name, address, and the date of birth. Some profiles could include a photograph of the customer. It is a database that would also have details of deposits made by gamblers and this could be seen by staff members working in the cage, other parts of the casino complexes and, more critically, the members of the anti-money laundering team responsible for monitoring and reporting suspect transactions.

Some entries in the customer relationship database recorded the aggregate of deposits for a particular gambler but other records had both the aggregate and individual deposit amounts recorded in the comment field. The inconsistency in recording meant that the team responsible for policing the financial conduct of the casino was unable to clearly see what was going on. Transactions hitting the bank accounts were not being recorded in the same manner in the customer database and that meant links between the two could not easily be made. Keeping Crown compliant and clean from a regulatory standpoint was not going to be easy with inconsistent record keeping and monitoring practices.

A consultancy called Initialism made this point in its recommendations to Crown in a 2019 draft report that was referred to in both the Bergin and Finkelstein reports. Initialism's draft report said that transaction monitoring across Crown needed to be automated rather than manual in order for the team responsible to be able to add value to the risk management program within Crown rather than worrying about how best to assemble the information it needed to understand what was happening. The draft report also noted that there were a number of people in different groups involved in fulfilling transaction monitoring and that created the possibility of duplication and inefficiency. Both Crown Melbourne and Crown Perth were told to improve their processes so that money laundering matters could monitored with greater precision at an enterprise level.

Monitoring of the accounts was also at the centre of concerns held by AUSTRAC when the body Matters also began to get complicated with AUSTRAC in 2016 when the anti-money laundering regulatory body decided meaningful discussions were in order with Crown regarding the possibility for the Southbank entity to become a reporting entity because of its activities. Internal legal advice described the activities of Southbank as merely being a conduit for the Crown business and it was determined that the entity would not be reporting in its own right to the anti-money laundering regulator. An implication of this is that the Southbank entity accounts would not be visible to AUSTRAC so that it could map how things made their way to Crown's internal systems.

Evidence of money laundering

Evidence tendered to the Bergin inquiry exposed methods used by a money changer to deposit amount from different bank branches, but those amounts were under the threshold of $10,000. Imagine the shoe leather the money changer had to wear out in order to avoid having tellers in one bank branch connecting the dots and coming up with a basis to report the money changer for engaging in activity that smells like money laundering. The ANZ began to drill down with questions about the bank account held by Riverbank in January 2014—which was not long after HSBC had flicked the Crown entities as banking customers—in order to get answers about why the account appeared to have so many transactions going from it to Burswood Casino's account.

A letter sent from the ANZ to Crown's Travis Costin stated that there had been an internal investigation that the account had received multiple deposits on the same day from different locations by the same person for amounts between $8,000 to $9,000. Crown's manager asked for further details and a spreadsheet was forthcoming from the bank that showed the transactions as well as images of deposit slips. An email tendered to the Bergin inquiry showed evidence of Costin telling a Crown insider that he felt he had talked the ANZ around to Crown's way of thinking. 'I just had a meeting with ANZ to discuss some transactions that occurred through Riverbank Investments, specifically money changers putting in multiple transactions,' Costin said in a 3 February 2014 email. 'I got ANZ comfortable around the accounts, but the one outstanding question was why the money changer deposits multiple amounts under $10k at different branches.' Disaggregating a larger amount of money by depositing it with different branches was clearly a red flag to the ANZ that laundering of funds was happening through Crown accounts. Bergin concluded in her report that it appeared nobody at Crown took the initiative to review the Riverview account balance to properly assess whether structuring was occurring.

It took only a few months into the commercial relationship between Crown and the ANZ for Crown's practices in relation to the Riverbank account to get the ANZ nervous. HSBC turfed Crown the year before, and the ANZ gave Crown notice that it would close the Riverbank accounts in July 2014. Costin wrote to staff members in Crown telling them that the ANZ had decided to pull the pin on the bank accounts and that Crown was not keen to have the same occur with new Commonwealth Bank accounts that were established. 'The closure of the Riverbank accounts was expected… can customers be advised by relevant people that multiple cash deposits in branch under the $10,0000 reporting threshold will not be accepted in the new CBA accounts, as we don't want this process to occur again with CBA in six months' time deciding to close the Riverbank and Southbank accounts due to the suspect transactions,' Costin said.

Costin's hope that the CBA would not close the accounts would eventually disappear because the inevitable happened once word got out into media reporting about the use of the accounts of Riverbank and Southbank entities for deposits of funds that reeked of organised crime activity. Numerous meetings were held between the CBA and senior figures at Crown with the bank telling the Crown executives that their commercial relationship was over. Crown's representatives were told during a meeting held on 27 August 2019 that there were a range of issues raised for the bank by the media coverage and that investigations by the bank into the accounts unearthed information that could not be shared with Crown. A further meeting on 4 October 2019 attended by Crown representatives with the CBA brought the news that the CBA was dropping the guillotine on the Southbank and Riverbank accounts. That relationship was over.

Problems in the land of the long white cloud

The CBA and the ANZ were not the only banks to give the Crown resorts the old heave-ho with a CBA subsidiary known as ASB Bank in New Zealand raising questions back in 2018 about Crown's accounts with them. A battery of queries was sent to Crown by executives from the ASB Bank asking very similar question to the kind that Crown had been confronted with in other circumstances. Were the accounts overseen by the board and senior management? Were they a part of the Crown Casino anti-money laundering program and audit process? A transaction relationship manager from the ASB Bank sought to have a conversation with Costin as a part of due diligence on the Southbank account. Crown took just under three months to respond to the ASB Bank but the responses that were provided to the ASB Bank were characterised by Bergin as being misleading where the detailed monitoring of transactions was concerned. 'There were serious shortcomings in the transaction monitoring of the Southbank and Riverbank accounts,' Bergin said. 'There is no evidence to support the suggestion that Crown made source of funds enquiries in respect of deposits into the Southbank and Riverbank accounts.' Crown misrepresented the extent of board level involvement in oversight of these accounts—a majority of the board knew nothing of them—and the extent to which the accounts were monitored by Crown itself when the funds hit Crown's own accounts. The ASB Bank also wrapped up their commercial relationships not long after they were unable to get answers from Crown that were to their satisfaction where account monitoring for the prevalence of money laundering was concerned.

Money laundering inside Crown

The focus up to this point has been the use of special accounts for the transfer of funds that were clearly coming from people who had a need to be protected from the curiosity of law enforcement and, frankly, authorities in their own jurisdiction. Another form of money laundering—direct exchange of cash for gambling chips in the casino—was reported widely in the media, throughout the inquiries as well as in the political realm with anti-gambling politician Andrew Wilkie. It was Wilkie who had brought the three instances of money laundering to the public view with the publication of footage showing money being exchanged for another consideration at the casino.

One instance from December 2017 showed an individual taking out cash that is said to have equalled many thousands of dollars from a bag with a cashier handing over plaques—a kind of gambling chip. The cashier then counts they amount they were given. A second incident shows chips being placed on a Suncity cash desk in exchange for cash. The patron appears on film as if they are giving staff a tip. The third piece of vision show an individual placing a cooler back on a cash counter in the Suncity room. Bundles of fifty-dollar notes are unpacked and placed neatly in stacks on the table. 'There is no issue in respect of the content of that footage. It is stark. It is obvious. It is clear that hundreds of thousands of dollars of cash was transported into the casino in shopping bags in these incidents,' Bergin said. 'The cash was exchanged for chips and plaques at the Suncity desk and the money was counted in a money counter on the Suncity desk. It appears that no checks were made as to the source of the cash.' The Bergin treatise on Crown's ills also noted that there was nothing in the form of identification that appeared to be provided to the staff at the desk but this may be that the individuals depositing funds or taking chips or plaques were known to the staff.

Video evidence published by Wilkie was not the only source relied upon by those conducting inquiries into Crown. There were also still photographs from security footage that showed there was a fair amount of money exchanged in this particular room. Switching cash for chips or some other good or service is a classic way of putting what appeared to be tainted or dirty money into a system for a bit of a clean.

Crown's senior management took note of the fact that there was curious conduct taking place in the Suncity room and Indran Subramaniam, Crown's Vice President International Business Operations, and Maguire met with the team running the Suncity room to ensure they had no more than $100,000 petty cash in the room. Subramaniam discovered upon informing staff working in the Suncity section of Crown that they had a heck of a lot more in the way of funds within that particular area of the casino. 'Mr Subramaniam discussed the new controls with the staff of Suncity and was informed by them that they had approximately $5.3 million in cash in the various drawers and cupboards at the Suncity desk,' the Bergin report noted. 'This money was counted by Mr Subramanian and other Crown staff and placed in "cage bags".' Staff checked other drawers at the Suncity cash desk following Subramaniam's instructions and there was another $300,000 in that room. Subramaniam had contact with police investigators in relation to the sums found in the Suncity quarters as well as doing another audit of the Suncity facilities to ensure that the new rules related to cash limits in the high roller facility were adhered to by staff. He found that they were.

What these instances in the video and the subsequent actions of Crown management demonstrate is that steps were taken to tighten internal controls when it became apparent that there needed to be a tightening of processes and procedures. Bergin's report observes that that it is unclear whether the large sums of cash that were seen in the Suncity premises at Crown were the proceeds of crime or just money that was undeclared but that there were 'very real concerns that the money taken from the suitcase and the shopping bags was more probably than not money that was to be laundered'. Bergin also nudged the readers of her report and observers of her inquiry into the realm of the rarely exercised discipline of critical thought. Casinos such as Crown might be vulnerable to money laundering given the amount of cash that goes through them but it does not automatically mean that every large amount of money being frittered about is being laundered.

MACHINE FIDDLES

While Crown Melbourne's position throughout this process was that the Gaming Machine Trial did not require the prior approval of the Commission, Crown Melbourne respects the Commission's decision, which brings this matter to a close.

Crown Resorts Media Release, 27 April 2018

This is the largest fine the Commission has issued to Crown and reflects the seriousness with which it considers the matter.

Victorian Commission for Gambling and Liquor Regulation, 27 April 2018

Crown's Melbourne casino was hit with a $300,000 fine from the gaming regulator in April 2018 when it was discovered that it had engaged in a trial during two months in 2017 involving what is known as 'button blanking'. The blanking of buttons involved the use of blanking plates on 17 pokies that would remove certain betting options from players and leaving them with a minimum and maximum betting option.

The trial got the company into hot water with the Victorian Commission for Gaming and Liquor Regulation because the blanking out of betting options was considered a variation or modification to gaming machines on the casino floor that required approval from the gaming regulator. The casino failed to nicely ask for permission to blank out buttons on 17 of the 2,628 machines that it had at that time and as such it was deemed by the Commission to have broken the law.

Crown copped the fine, which was the highest issued to Crown at the time, as well as a letter of censure. The letter of censure was not simply advising Crown that they had been naughty and to cough up the funds. It also contained within it a requirement that Crown update its compliance framework within the space of six months and to explain to the regulator how a revised framework would prevent buttons being blanked in a similar fashion at the Melbourne venue.

The media release issued by the regulator also had a shopping list of factors the regulator considered when deciding what punishment to mete out to the casino, which had no history of disciplinary action being taken against it for electronic gaming machine matters before this occasion, for experimenting with button blanking on less than one per cent of its total number of gaming machines.

Crown cooperated with the investigation, according to the regulator, and the contravention was not one that was deliberate, but made by a small cohort of staff who thought regulatory approval was not necessary. They failed to talk to others within the business before the trial kicked off. The company moved quickly to pull the pin on the trial when the issue was brought to the company's attention and before the issue was even brought before the authorities for consideration. There was also the issue of there being no impact on the percentage of wagered funds that was paid back to the players that used the affected machines.

The factors mentioned above were ones that played in Crown's favour, but the regulator remained concerned about the seriousness of varying a machine for boost revenue to the casino without the relevant sign off from the regulator, and there was also the need to ensure there was a deterrent casino and other gaming venue operators from mucking about with electronic gaming machines in ways designed to get more revenue.

A witness to the Perth inquiry, James Sullivan, detailed his recollection of the button blanking fracas in an amended witness statement dated 9 August 2021. Sullivan's statement to the inquiry noted that he was approached by Crown's top brass to check whether similar practices were occurring in Perth. 'I recall receiving a phone call from Joshua Preston around the time that the issues arose in Melbourne,' Sullivan said. 'I recall Mr Preston saying that he would email me the detail of the allegations and asked me to review the nature of the allegations and advise him whether I considered any of the allegations had ever occurred in relation to EGM operations at Crown Perth as far as I was aware.'

Preston sent Sullivan a list of questions to which he required answers regarding the way in which the electronic gaming machines were being regulated at the casino in Perth. Sullivan told Preston that he did not recall any button blanking practices of the kind that took place in Melbourne taking place in Perth.

Evidence given by Sullivan to the Perth inquiry revealed that it was deemed necessary to conduct a review or audit of the installed gaming machines in the Perth casino to confirm that the casino did not engage in the button blanking practice. 'I believe I discussed this matter with Mr Kelly and requested he direct members of the Gaming Product team to conduct this review,' Sullivan said. 'I believe my team subsequently conducted the review and confirmed that no improper "button blanking" issues were identified.'

Sullivan's witness statement details the fact he participated in a in a meeting with other Crown Perth executives to discuss electronic gaming machine product issues so they better understood the way in which the gaming machine part of the business operated given the heightened level of attention that was being received by Crown Melbourne in relation to the button blanking issue.

Sullivan's witness statement further clarifies that there was no button blanking at the Perth casino that was designed to remove mid-level betting options. There were, however, likely to be blank buttons on the electronic gaming machines for other reasons. 'When the button panel of a gaming machine is set up, there are some approved configurations that do internationally blank certain button positions,' Sullivan explained. 'These buttons are not blanked at Crown Perth's discretion, but rather in accordance with the Accredited Test Facility certification as to how the game is approved and intended to operate. I am not aware of [buttons] ever being deliberately blanked at Crown Perth other than in this approved and intended way.'

Sullivan nevertheless complied with a request for a review of the machines at the Perth venue to ensure that there was no tampering or unintended configuration with buttons on the machines at the Perth Casino.

Public attention on button blanking

Crown and the regulator might have wrapped the issue up in April 2018 but allegations of tampering with machines had been tabled in Federal Parliament by Andrew Wilkie, the member for Denison in the House of Representatives. Wilkie has been in contact with whistleblowers who had notified him of the issue related to the modification of buttons on electronic gaming machines. He told the House of Representatives that allegations were brought to him by former Casino employees and related to issues of concern regarding not just the behaviour of Crown Casino but other players in the poker or electronic gaming machine space. 'The whistleblowers allege illegal machine tampering, including the disabling of lower-bet options and the modifying of buttons to allow prohibited autoplay, both of which increase gambler losses,' Wilkie said. 'Moreover, there's software manipulation to increase gambler losses even further, in particular, on weekends when the number of naive, first-time and casual users is obviously much greater.' Wilkie expressed concern that the gambling regulator in Victoria appeared to have done nothing about 'shocking criminal misconduct' and that the whistleblowers said they believed the regulator itself was in the business of covering misconduct up.

Wilkie tabled a video of whistleblowers in parliament on this occasion in order to put the allegations on the record. 'You will see that the identities of the whistleblowers have been obscured for their personal safety, and because it was a condition of them speaking out,' Wilkie said. 'However, their identities have been confirmed by me, and I'm confident we must consider very seriously the information they provide. These whistleblowers know the risks they're taking by speaking up. I pay tribute to them for doing this.'

Wilkie called on governments, law enforcement and regulatory agencies to take the allegations seriously. This would not be the only time Wilkie would comment on Crown and a series of media releases on Melbourne casino related issues would be issued by him until the various inquiries looking into Crown were under way.

Stimulating autoplay

One of the issues related to the poker machines that was raised by Wilkie was the use of methods to stimulate autoplay, which was prohibited in the casinos. Machines are designed to be played by patrons one press at a time but some clients use picks, bank cards, and other things to try to keep the buttons down to play the games continuously. There was a period when Crown picks were distributed to patrons to help them keep buttons down to stimulate autoplay but this was, according to evidence given to the Finskelstein Royal Commission by Crown executive Mark Mackay, discontinued in 2018. Mackay said that it was common for people in higher membership levels at Crown to use picks or similar devices for autoplay. 'I think across the tiers it is probably more common in the higher-level tiers, as in black, and less common in the lower tiers gold and below,' Mackay said. 'Platinum and black, and gold and below would be less common.'

Mackay also noted that once people stopped being given the Crown picks for the purposes of autoplay they were 'discouraged' from continuing stimulating autoplay although it was not necessarily a policy document that drove that development. 'I don't think it was part of a document or policy. It was communicated to the teams that operate in the VIP areas,' Mackay said. 'I think the policy or memo, if it's not a policy, but the memo specifically said to reclaim the Crown pick and discourage the customers from playing a gaming machine that way, but I have to again review that document.' It was put to Mackay by counsel assisting the Finkelstein royal commission that an observer could conclude that the reason Crown personnel were asked to get patrons to cease using the Crown picks was reputation risk management rather than concern about patron's gambling habits. Mackay agreed that the practice of discouraging patrons from engaging in autoplay could be seen that way.

Mackay was also quizzed on the issue of patrons playing multiple machines at once, which was against general policies related to using electronic gaming machines on the premises. Counsel assisting was told by Mackay that staff were asked to ensure people stopped playing more than one. 'We issued a direction to the main gaming floor Riverside team to ensure that if they see anyone playing multiple machines, to ask the customer to stop playing multiple machines,' Mackay said. 'In the Teak and Mahogany Rooms customers—some of our customers have access to an ancillary card and therefore some choose to play multiple machines at the same time. That still is an allowed practice in those premium rooms.'

Mackay was further grilled about the consistency of the various practices used by Crown in the electronic gaming machine facilities with the encouragement of responsible gambling. He told counsel assisting that a wealthy person might enjoy gambling on multiple machines and not do too much damage to their financial position. Counsel assisting was not done with Mackay given the evidence of the Crown employee had only dealt with the gambling habits of people with enough money to cushion the blow of losses. Mackay confirmed that Crown had only recently begun looking into the financial circumstances of their patrons. Counsel assisting took it a step further. 'So if you don't know what their financial circumstances are, do you agree with me that if one were to prioritise the welfare of Victorians, you wouldn't have a practice that allowed people to have picks or other devices that depressed the play button, and you wouldn't allow multiple play on multiple EGMs at once?' counsel assisting asked. Mackay agreed.

There were a series of other problems that were noted by the Finkelstein report related to the way in which the Melbourne Casino maintained its electronic gaming machines. A list in an appendix to the report states that there were errors identified in poker machine identification, touchscreen errors were found among other general machine errors, machines operated without the correct time on their displays for nine hours, a report of five poker machines being below the required luminance level, and incorrect payouts from machines. The issues raised provide a sense of the granularity into which the Finkelstein juggernaut went into looking at the way in which Crown as an institution deal with administering poker machines.

SEE PHIL COLLINS FOR $30,000

Used to go into the casino as a 17-year-old, looked a bit more mature than my age so I was never questioned for ID, so it was quite easy to go in and just get addicted to the casino lifestyle and the atmosphere.

Ahmad Hasna, small business owner and problem gambler

The Commission has examples of the kinds of communications that members received from hosts. Some of these were plainly directed towards emotionally manipulating customers into spending more money for the benefit of their hosts.

Ray Finkelstein, Royal Commissioner

In summary, the job of the host is 'to get people to come in and gamble no matter what'.

Ray Finkelstein, Royal Commissioner

Would a diehard fan pay $30,000 to go and see Phil Collins, the man responsible for hits such as *In the Air Tonight* and *Against All Odds*, live in concert? It turns out that one man did pay that much and he was not even a Collins fan. Small business owner Ahmad Hasna got the concert tickets as a part of the service Crown Casino offered to their high worth gamblers. Hasna was gambling tens of thousands at a time. When his Crown host, the title given to those that have clients whose needs they must look after, offered free tickets to a Phil Collins gig, Hasna did not refuse them but had to go into the venue to pick them up. It was here that the prized client of Crown 'dropped' $30,000 on one of the gambling tables on the same day he picked the tickets up. The host had done their job. Investment in the Collins tickets had given them the chance to hoover more money out of Hasna's pockets. That bet paid off and the house won.

Hasna's gambling journey

Hasna's gambling addiction did not develop overnight. His interest in games of chance began in his teens. He started gambling at the age of 17 and for many years he found gambling to be a form of entertainment with Crown Casino being the beneficiary of this view. Hasna's gambling activity grew as he got older and at some stage after completing a qualification he was gambling for up to six hours at Crown for five days a week. He told the royal commission that when he began gambling in his teens he was sneaking into Crown Casino and successfully getting past security because he looked older but at times security guards got wise and sought ID. Multiple entry points to the casino meant that any attempt to kick him out of the venue failed.

This was Hasna's introduction to gambling, during which he was not throwing too much money about. 'I didn't have the funds and the power to play at the level which I ended up playing at, but as I moved on to my adult life, probably I would say since the—oh, probably say at the age of 25, once I'd become an adult and graduated through university and was in charge of the family business and was having access to larger amount of sums is when I would become a more frequent visitor and a player,' Hasna said. His perception of the Casino, as a form of entertainment, according to the evidence he delivered before the Finkelstein inquiry changed as time moved on and he lost more money.

Hasna's preferred gambling outlet was the roulette table but he avoided the poker machines. He had spent enough at the roulette table to get himself to the prized black card holder status that resulted in getting a host that would handle all contact with the casino. Want a room at the hotel? The host handled it. A restaurant booking at the casino complex? Just ask the host to fix it and it happened. Hansa also used his black card holder status to help mates—also black card holders—get a table at restaurants because the amount they played at the casino was deemed to be insufficient and therefore the level of service they received was lower.

'You might have problems, say, with maybe not being able to park in certain areas when valet parking is full, so your host can pretty much waive a lot of—and give you a lot of exemptions to a lot of things,' Hasna said. 'Basically, having a host and a host that is powerful can waive a lot of rules for you.' A host, according to Hasna, had no rules with which they had to comply, and restaurant bookings made by the host usually meant that the gambler was not paying. 'Numerous occasions I would book the top-end restaurants at Nobu or all the other seafood restaurants because we enjoy eating, and especially if you don't have to pay,' Hasna told the commission. The host had no limitations when it came to satisfying a gambler holding a black card membership—provided a gambler like Hasna continued to allow Crown to hoover up his cash.

No such thing as a free lunch

Black card holders were pampered to the point of no return and Crown's hosts knew precisely what they were doing. Hasna told the commission that he was one of the casino's top five local gamblers and they threw free tickets to shows and sporting events at him. Phil Collins was on tour at one point in time and Hasna went into the Casino to pick the tickets up. 'I'm not a Phil Collins fan, but I still took them because they give them out,' Hasna said. 'You know, sometimes on that occasion I got called in to pick up Phil Collins tickets, because you got to go in and pick them up, I went in to pick them up and I dropped $30,000. So going in to pick up Phil Collins tickets cost me $30,000 for my friends that went to watch him.' Hasna learned over time that there was no such thing as a free lunch and being lured into the venue to collect tickets to a Phil Collins concert was one such example.

Crown's hosts were not the only ones that would monitor a gambler's progress at various tables. Hasna told Finkelstein and the counsel assisting the inquiry that there were pit bosses at tables monitoring whether the games were being played properly and that the dealers were paying out correctly. There would also be the communication with the money men at the casinos in the cage when somebody would win and need to cash it in. That would be communicated via an electronic device so that people handling the pay outs to the punters knew what to expect. Payouts were recorded accurately, but Finkelstein asked Hasna whether the amount that was being gambled was accurately recorded. Hasna said that some of the money lost at the casino would have been recorded but there was no way everything he lost was documented.

'So, for example, I would put $2,000 on a table to get gaming chips. They would record that against your membership,' Hasna said. 'So they do keep a record, but it's not an accurate record where it's 100 per cent accurate of what you lost and won'. Hasna also revealed that there were times when he would leave the casino with several thousands of dollars' worth of chips, and that he was not even concerned about security. 'I've gone home with $3,000 or $4,000 in chips and I've just kept them at home, and then I come back the next day,' Hasna told Finkelstein. 'You are never questioned in terms of leaving the premises with their gaming chips. That's never an issue.'

Hasna was also not asked for identification when he was seeking to exchange cash for gambling chips at the mahogany room. The high rollers hidey hole in Crown would not ask for identification for exchanges of funds while Hasna was playing there unless the amounts being asked for in chips exceeded $10,000 in one transaction. 'You're not asked for ID, you could go away, play, lose that money, come back again, cash another $9,000. So as long as you don't exceed the $10,000, you are never really asked for ID,' Hasna said. 'But at the actual gaming table, you can cash whatever money you like, you are never questioned.'

The treatment for the high-profile gambler would eventually change when he began to gamble on the smell of an oily rag.

Where did the money come from?

How did Hasna gamble and become such an important pampered client for Crown? He typically gambled alone for a range of reasons. Hansa told the royal commission that there was a sense of shame he felt when he would play with money as if it meant nothing to him while for friends and family it would be something about which they would feel agonised.

'I always just went alone. And the amount of visits I did it was pretty hard to bring anyone with you, because it was long hours,' Hasna said. 'It was like a shift. It was like a shift worker, pretty much.'

Finkelstein raised questions about how somebody in Hasna's position could justify losses of $100,000 and where the money came from to satiate the impulses to continue gambling. The answer, according to Hasna, was to find a way to get more money to continue to chase losses and to do that he had to lie to people with whom he had a relationship rather than going through a bank.

'You have to be a good liar in terms of obtaining that cash. It's all borrowed funds,' Hasna explained. 'It's funds that I borrow through family and friends.' He had a profile and reputation with family and friends at the time his gambling addiction was at his peak and he somehow managed to squeeze more money from people. 'Being in the industry that we are in, a lot of our sales and our—a contract is just a word of mouth for us in the industry we deal in,' Hasna said 'I will tell you an example, five of these cars, yeah, no problem, transfer a hundred, they will transfer a hundred before you even send the cars across. That is how the debt accumulates.' Those people handing him the money were clearly under the impression the cash was needed for a legitimate business reason. 'A lot of people lending you money don't know why. They assume it is for a business purpose,' Hasna said. 'But 99 per cent of the time it wasn't for business purposes, it was for gambling, the habit.' This approach meant that Hasna would on his own admission wind up with between $5 million to $6 million in debt at the time he gave evidence at the royal commission.

The debt accumulated by Hasna had consequences for his participation in the family business. Crown's favourite gambler was stripped by his family of any authorisation to sign financial documents. Family and friends became concerned about his gambling habits, and Hasna's brother played a role in elbowing him to the side when money matters were concerned. 'It is a family business and quite early on, my brother is my partner and discovered my addictions I had, and I was removed very, very quickly from anything that was of value in terms of being able to make any decisions or have control of any family funds,' Hasna said. This meant that cheques were cancelled and chequebooks were cancelled and Hasna admitted to the royal commission that he had lost respect from his family and his community because the rate at which his addition was chewing up cash led to questions needing to be asked. Hasna ended up selling his home because of his gambling habit.

Self-exclusion

Hasna signed up twice to the self-exclusion scheme at Crown Casino that he characterised as being rather basic and simple. He declared he had problems with gambling to Crown in 2012 and 2015 and that meant he effectively spent a year away from the Crown premises. The self-exclusion process requires a person to see a psychologist specialising in gambling problems three times over three months. The self-excluding gambler had to find a counsellor with expertise in gambling and attend sessions for which the gambler paid. Hasna told Finkelstein that he went to the counsellor to get back into gambling rather than to stay away from the addictive climate. '[It was] very basic counselling, and I think maybe the system failed in a way to identify, was this person trying to go in because, like you said, trying to seek to get back in, or did he really need counselling,' Hasna said. 'In my case I needed to get back in because it is an addiction that I had that hadn't been cured.'

Permanent ban from Crown

In December 2019 the relationship Hasna had with Crown Casino came to an end. He'd gotten to the point where he was 'running off fumes' and he was unable to get his hands on cash through his usual contacts. The host with whom Hasna had a relationship was asked to arrange a holiday, given that Hasna had no money to pay for a family holiday. They were sent to Burswood over in Perth and Hasna managed to find a way of securing $50,000 at gambling tables on what was meant to be a family holiday. He had a run in with the hotel manager when questioned whether they were hotel guests despite the fact that Crown Melbourne—more specifically the host that pandered to every need Hasna requested—had organised the holiday.

'So [the hotel manager] was under the assumption that maybe we had snuck in to use the hotel facility. I said that 'Yeah, I am definitely a guest staying in your hotel.' And a couple of minutes later she sent security towards me again, and again they were questioning whether we were guests at the hotel or not,' Hasna said. 'At that stage, after losing $50,000 in your casino, words were going to be exchanged because obviously I was quite distressed and pissed off.' The family left early the next day without having breakfast at the hotel and a senior management figure, Peter Lawrence, told Hasna he was not welcome in their casino properties for 12 months because of the altercation with security staff in Perth.

Peter Lawrence called Hasna again, according to the evidence delivered by Hasna, when Crown's woes became more public and their pampered class of gambler was being told that they were excluded. Hasna told the royal commission that Lawrence told him during the call that he was permanently excluded from the casino, it was not just a one-year ban for him to cool his heels. This one was forever and Hasna told Finkelstein the ban was definitely in place. There was no way, the former holder of the black card at Crown said, that he would not be noticed. 'Security all know me. I've had such a long history and run in with security. In terms of surveillance when you are playing, I'm like Santa Claus when I walk in there because they know what I look like and the level of play and the way I play,' Hasna said. 'So within five minutes of going in I'd be escorted out by security, and usually they don't escort you out in a polite way. They are quite aggressive.'

The cheque controversy

A key issues within the Finkelstein report was an incident involving Hasna and a $100,000 cheque that had him as the payee. This cheque was used by Hasna to get the equivalent dollar amount in gambling chips. Hasna proceeded to gamble and lose the lot. That cheque was dishonoured and Hasna was called by the Crown staffer, the host responsible for handling his account, and Hasna told his host he was in financial distress and unable to pay the debt. The addicted gambler told the host he was considering self-exclusion. The full report of the inquiry observes that the host had followed the instructions from Lawrence and advised Hasna that he could continue to play at Crown and maintain the privileges of his black card provided his debt was paid out of winnings. In other words, the casino had come up with a plan to keep Hasna at the tables and, frankly, it worked. Hansa played. Hasna repaid the debt. Repayment of that debt, however, did not stop Hasna from playing more and more, and losing more money as a result.

Lawrence was quizzed about this sequence of events during the hearings of the royal commission and was asked whether he thought Crown's behaviour in letting Hasna come back was 'predatory and irresponsible'. Lawrence initially agreed that the behaviour was irresponsible but he had to be pressed on the issue of whether he agreed the behaviour was predatory. 'Yes, it… it's a strong word, but possibly yes,' Lawrence said under examination.

Crown had another problem. The left hand had no idea what the right had was doing with regard to discussions with Hasna about his personal financial state. It appeared that Lawrence was unaware of the fact that the host in Crown had a discussion with Hasna about poor financial circumstances. 'I wasn't aware that Mr Hasna had advised his host that he was experiencing financial [difficulty] and was considering self-exclusion from Crown. I wasn't aware of that,' Lawrence said. This was a part of the culture of Crown's governance when it came to the high worth players and how those players were treated by the organisation that had a kitty ready to take their funds. Gamblers were not asked about the money they gambled. The hosts were not the ones to suggest self-exclusion. This included if somebody is wading knee deep in debt or had some other financial problems. Hosts were there to keep the sucker with the deep pockets and the supersized wallets coming in. Folks working in the Mahogany Room would not duck in to look at the wellbeing of people at the casino before they hit 12 hours of continuous play. There are also people that would play for 12 to 24 hours at a time. Hosts would do everything possible to get the gamblers back into the venue. Evidence taken from hosts that had worked at Crown revealed that the culture was about pulling in the money and worrying about responsible gambling issues as a secondary priority. 'It goes without saying, but it must be said, that it is inconsistent with the practice of responsible gambling for a casino to encourage a patron to gamble in the hope that the patron can win enough to discharge their debt to the casino,' the commissioner said in his report. 'Yet this is what happened with Mr Hasna.'

Finkelstein was still ruminating on his final report when Hasna decided to take Crown Casino to court. Documents were lodged with the Federal Court of Australia pursuing a case under consumer protection laws. Hasna has asserted in his court application that Crown had engaged in unconscionable conduct and also for breaking its own internal rules because they had sought to encourage Hansa to continue to gamble using a range of incentives such as holidays and tickets to events as well as betting on credit. He told the Court he was seeking almost $4.6 million in damages. The case was still in progress at the time of writing.

The Kakavas case

Hasna's court case against Crown is not the only legal tussle that the gambling giant has faced. Harry Kakavas was a prominent property developer who had the gambling bug. He had thrown a fair bit of coin at baccarat tables at Crown Casino. He was, according to court records, a pathological gambler and prone to spending and losing a bit of cash at the tables. Just a little, in fact. Kakavas managed to lose $20.5 million paying at the gaming tables between June 2005 and August 2006 at the same casino where he began to gamble back in June 1994. He lost $110,000 of his father's money that year and then defrauded Esanda Finance Corporation of approximately $286,000—a fraud that resulted in Kakavas serving four months in jail. The release from the clink saw him attempt to revoke a self-exclusion order that he had put into place with Crown in November 1995. That order was revoked in June 1998 but was then replaced by a withdrawal of licence to go into and remain in the casino because of pending armed robbery charges.

Kakavas was not given administrative clearance to re-enter Crown Casino until a decision was made by an internal Crown committee on 29 October 2004 that he should be able to enter Crown Casino given that he was gambling at Star City Casino in Sydney and also that he had been very successful in business. There were still hurdles for Kakavas to clear. A crown employee, Richard Doggett, spoke on the phone with Kakavas in December 2004 and told him that Crown was 'being very pedantic with your application' because he was excluded from other casinos and excluded by the Chief Commissioner of Police in New South Wales. There was even a letter given to Doggett, according to court documents, by Kakavas that same month that purported to be a letter from a psychologist providing Crown with an assessment of Kakavas' suitability to resume gambling at Crown. He was not assessed but psychologist Janine Brooks prepared a report that supported Kakavas return to the casino. Brooks said she was unable to assess Kakavas as being suitable for readmission, but she noted that Kakavas had said that he was a compulsive gambler between 1990 and 1998 but that he had turned his life around. Brooks' letter also noted that Kakavas had said he would implement a plan to self-exclude again if old habits re-emerged.

Crown revoked the withdrawal of license in January 2005 and invited Kakavas to the Australian Open that year and Crown negotiated benefits with him that included the use of their private jet, gambling rebates, accommodation for Kakavas and his guests as well as table limits for bets. Private jet travel was not going to be provided to Kakavas until he made more frequent visits to Crown. The judges said they observed the discussions between Crown and Kakavas showed that Kakavas was able to negotiation in his own interests. He did not re-enter Crown Casino until 24 June 2005 and between that date and 17 August 2006 he visited the venue 28 times and was involved in 30 different gambling programs. In other words, the judges sitting in the High Court saw Kakavas as somebody able to take care of his own affairs.

The High Court challenge

Kakavas decided to try and take Crown to task in the High Court because he argued that Crown had engaged in unconscionable conduct because it had not told him that any winnings he had were forfeiting because he had an interstate exclusion order that meant any winnings were withheld from him. Kakavas also argued in his case against Crown that they had incited him to gamble at its establishment by offering him rebates on losses and flights on the Crown corporate jet.

Kakavas took Crown to court once and then appealed a court judgement that went against him. He took the matter to the high court of Australia where he was given leave to appeal to take his case further. The case that was before the high Court had a different emphasis. Kakavas argued in the high court that Crown had exploited his inability to make decisions in his own interests while gambling given his addiction. A part of his argument before the high court was the fact that the initial trial judge and the court of appeal had failed because they considered the ability of Kakavas to bargain with

Crown rather than his decision-making being compromised because of addiction. 'The appellant submitted that because Crown knew of, or ought to have been aware of, the appellant's special disadvantages, or was sufficiently on notice of them to have been obliged, in accordance with notions of constructive notice, to make further inquiries concerning the appellant's circumstances, Crown ought now be made to disgorge its takings to the appellant,' the high court judgement said. Crown as the respondent in the high court case said that Kakavas was not in a position of special disadvantage that Crown sought to exploit. The gambling giant highlighted that Kakavas 'presented as successful businessman able to afford to indulge himself in the high stakes gambling in which he chose to engage', the High Court judgement explained. 'Crown employees accepted him as he sought to present himself.'

The high court's analysis of the fact pattern and the argument Kakavas sought to put forward was eviscerating. Kakavas, the high Court said, tried to argue that his case was unique and needed to be distinguished from the general business of Crown. The judges said it was difficult for them to find a special reason in the fact pattern presented to the court for them to conclude that Crown's responsibility should have gone beyond satiating Kakavas' demand to play at the tables and take on the risk of gambling. The judge's also noted that Kakavas actively chose to be at the casino—a choice he made many times—where he could lose money at the tables playing his chosen games. This conformed with the notion that gambling was an activity in which both parties involved in the are trying to outsmart the other. 'Gambling transactions are a rare, if not unique, species of economic activity in a civilised community, in that each party sets out openly to inflict harm on the counterparty,' the judges said. 'In the language of Lord Hardwicke, there was nothing 'surreptitious' about Crown's conduct. Kakavas ultimately lost the High Court attempt that brought an end to several years of legal brawling with the casino.

A lesson from Hayne

There are times when contacts of gambling addicted people need to conduct an intervention to ensure that their friends, family member, and even employees take steps to end their gambling addiction that leads to debt. This can sometimes mean that the person who was caught up in the clutches of a gambling addition needed help to turn off the pipeline of funds. In a prominent case study from the royal commission into misconduct in the financial services sector, helmed by Kenneth Hayne, the employer of a gambling addicted tradesman, David Harris, made the effort to go to a Commonwealth Bank branch to ensure his employee shut down credit cards that were assisting in the maintenance of a gambling habit. The bank had failed to ensure its systems captured the fact Harris had told them he was a gambling addict and as such he kept getting additional credit. Harris is a roofer by trade and came to Australia at the age of 25 on a 457 visa in January 2013 that enabled him to work in the country. He got his first credit card with a limit of $10,000 in order to have money available while traveling to Thailand for a dental operation and for hotel expenditure. It was on his return to Australia in February 2015 that he repaid the initial debt on the card but he began gambling on credit rather than using his own money, as he had done up to that point.

Harris had maxed-out the initial card later in 2015 and that started him on his journey of debt the Commonwealth Bank had begun. Credit card limits of $10,000 turned into $12,000 and eventually over a year the credit limit ended up being $27,000 thanks to the fact that Harris had got himself three separate cards. It was in April 2016 that he was persuaded by a bank staffer to consolidate three cards into one with no change in the credit limit. 'I banked some money at a cash point and it didn't—sometimes it goes—automatically straight into your account, and it hadn't gone in so I rang up the bank to find out why it hadn't gone in,' Harris told the Commission, 'and then the woman started asking why I had three credit cards, saying that they could consolidate into one, so I would—rather than paying the three different lots—rates of interest, they would put it on to my lower rate card so I was paying the lower rate of interest.'

It was in October 2016 that Harris ended up telling the bank he had a gambling problem and as such he did not want to increase the credit limit any further. Harris' wish to not receive an increase in credit on the basis he told them he was a gambling addict was not recorded and the bank bumped it up again from $27,000 to $32,000 and with another $3,000 to $35,000. His employer ended up providing him with funds to pay off the credit card as well as going to the branch with him to get it shut down. This ended up being in vain when Harris was shuffled between customer service representatives in a branch and on a phone. He cut the card up, didn't use credit for several months but then requested a replacement card. Harris incurred debt again and ended up being chased for debt repayments by the Commonwealth Bank. Harris had negotiated a hardship agreement and a payment plan with the bank but various bank officers continued to contact him for information he had already supplied.

There was a dilemma for a corporate entity such as a bank in dealing with a client's circumstances where they involved legal activities such as gambling. Clive van Horen, a CBA executive that appeared before the Hayne Royal Commission, said that there was a problem when the purchase of legal goods and services was concerned. 'You can quickly see the slippery slope that puts us on if we say you can't spend on gambling. Well, then what about other, you know, addictive spending on shopping or on alcohol or any other causes?' he said. 'So, you know, this is what we've grappled with. Absent any clear legal or regulatory guideline, how do we determine when we intervene and impose limits?'

The Commonwealth Bank found itself in the cross hairs of the corporate regulator and also the Federal Court over this case study from the Hayne Royal Commission involving a problem gambler. Failing to take account of the fact that the bank was told by Harris that he was a problem gambler got them into the Federal Court of Australia. The Justice Murphy of the Federal Court found that the bank failed to inquire into Harris' gambling problems and his broader financial situation before bumping up the credit limit from $27,000 to $35,000 on 20 January 2017. 'ASIC alleged and CBA admitted that this misconduct was the result of inadequate systems and processes in respect of problem gambler notifications,' a statement released by the corporate regulator said on 30 October 2020. 'Because of these inadequacies, CBA failed to take account of Mr Harris' notification that he was a problem gambler and to take reasonable steps to verify his financial situation before offering and approving a credit card limit increase.'

CROOKS, JUNKETS AND JAILS

The aggressive pursuit of profit was favoured to the disregard of the welfare of the employees in China.

The Bergin Report, February 2021

It is the case that Crown dealt with many international junket operators evidenced in part by the fact that when it ceased its operations in China from November 2016 it terminated its relationships with over 100 junket operators in Mainland China.

The Bergin Report, February 2021

There was a time when Crown Casino appeared to be fond of any dollar that it could find to pop into its burgeoning kitty. Crown operatives would spend their time in Australia and overseas looking at ways of bringing people with fat wallets and bank accounts through Crown's doors. This included seeking gamblers from overseas jurisdictions who would be happy to drop their dollars on the gaming tables and at the poker machines at Crown's venues. These games came with high stakes and those high stakes were not simply faced by the players spending their money at the venue. Crown itself knew it walked on the fine, sharp edge of a blade in the service of a profit-based objective when promoting their business overseas. This included staff hawking crown's venue in China getting themselves imprisoned as well as there being junkets that were a method of organising obscenely rich individuals with deep pockets to rock up to one of Crown's venues, spill cash on a table and then to go back home. These junkets brought with them a motherlode. Counsel assisting Finkelstein's Crown deep dive said that that the casino made 'hundreds of millions of dollars in revenue from junkets between 2017 and 2019'.

Junkets are basically the equivalent of a package tour for obscenely rich individuals that want to fritter away their hard earned at a gambling venue. These arrangements would involve a junket operator and the casino coming to an agreement that would result in people with deep pockets rocking into town, dumping their cash, and then leaving. The process of getting a tour with people desperate to throw their money at a gambling venue would also involve the provision of specialised chips that equalled the amount of money that provided as 'front money'. The guests play away and once a program ends it is up to the casino to determine whether the junket beat the house. There is a need for the casino nut out the amount of tax that is required to be paid resulting from transactions related to the junket. Junket tours pose another problem for a venue. They are a way in which a casino may find itself—knowingly or unknowingly—dealing with people that have linkages with organised crime. This means that the junket process could be used as a way of laundering money by crooked individuals or a means of rich folks shuffling money out of a jurisdiction that might have certain limits on how much money can be pushed out the door. The only way that the casino operator could hope to avoid such entanglements with organised crime running junkets is to do due diligence and try to ensure as best as they can the guests brought in by the junket tour operator were clean. The other way of avoiding headaches with junkets is to not run them at all.

Crown's international operations

Crown had spent significant resource to target what they called VIP high roller players across the Asian region and that it had, according to its 2008 Annual Report, built a database of targets. The focus of on high rollers was something Crown marketed as being a strong point for the gambling behemoth because high rollers that visited remained loyal because of their satisfaction with the gaming facilities and client services. The high reputation that Crown's executives spoke of was run by what it called the VIP International Unit. It was this business unit that managed overseas venues that Crown had as well as having the responsibility to develop relationships with gamblers with bucketloads of money to throw around in order to convince them that they should drop by to Australia. Chasing money by chasing high rollers was done by a team of people flogging the Crown product in countries such as Malaysia, Thailand, China and Singapore. Members of the sales team were focused on both sourcing new VIP players as well as focusing on junkets and boosting the revenue from both sources. Operators of junkets in Hong Kong and Macau were also targeted by VIP International.

A familiar identity, James Packer in his role as chairman of Crown, used his profile and leverage during the period between 2007 to 2015 to try and help build the junket business. The Packer influence on trying to grow the high roller business—even treble it—by using Crown's links in Macao was critical. Packer's involvement in the international business of Crown was very cosy and the Bergin report noted that it was Packer's expectation while he was chairman of the entity that senior executives working within the international business unit at Crown informed him of important issues related to the international business. Did this always occur? Not necessarily. Significant issues related to Chinese police questioning a Crown staffer in Wuhan in July 2015 were not communicated to Packer by management.

Junkets might have been seen as a way of getting money into the coffers of the Crown establishments in Australia, but numerous problems presented themselves with the junket tour organisers Crown had dealings with because of links to organised crime. Could Crown have done more to drill down into the operators and the players they were bringing out? Reports into Crown's administration of junkets lead to the inevitable conclusion that more could have been done with admissions from members of the board of directors that processes could have been improved. Crown was the subject of disciplinary action in December 2017 by the Victorian casino regulator when it was found it had failed to properly document relevant details of junkets as well as the identities of individuals and amounts of funds. A fine of $150,000 for failure to properly document arrangements in 13 cases was the regulator flexing muscles, but that fine would have been a drop in a bucket considering the tens of millions Crown's accounts were reflecting.

The junket operators exposed in public

Seven junket operators with alleged criminal histories were looked at closely in the context of the Bergin inquiry. A further question was whether Crown knew about the criminal histories at the time and what it did when those links were established. Bergin's laundry list of the seven junket operators and their operations is eye opening for anyone unfamiliar with the magnetic appeal that casinos have to those with criminal intent.

The Company, which was the first of the junkets named in media reports, was known for dealings in truck trafficking and money laundering. Crown was unable to connect the Company and its criminal background with junket operators with which it was dealing until global media reports described The Company or the Sam Gor

Syndicate as a grouping of five Chinese triads that was associated with the trafficking of illicit drugs in Australia. Tse Chi Lop was reported in a Reuters article published in October 2019 as being the leader of the Sam Gor Syndicate. A second operator Roy Moo, a representative of a junket operator from 1997 to 2013, got caught laundering money and wound up behind bars in 2013 for that little enterprise he undertook to launder the proceeds of crime for The Company. He was caught on camera collecting the big bucks in a shopping bag. Bergin's report observed that Crown would have been able to link the existence of The Company following the publication in October 2019 of the Reuters article and corroborating the story it told with casino regulator's sixth review of Crown casino.

A case study contained in that particular review referred to the Sam Gor Syndicate. Tse Chi Lop was arrested in in the Netherlands on 22 January 2021 and was awaiting extradition at the time the Bergin report was published to face charges related to drug importation into Australia. A third junket operator Ng Chi Un operated a junket called the Hot Pot Junket that was described as being linked to organised crime groups. Tse Chi Lop is referred to as a 'suspected silent partner' in a Macau-based restaurant business called Hot Pot. Crown did acknowledge that it was unable to satisfy itself that the operator of the Hot Pot Junket was 'good repute'.

Suncity and the operator of that junket, Alvin Chau, were also a part of the mix when it came to the inquiring minds among the counsel assisting Bergin and Finkelstein and the tyre kicking exercise they embarked on to test how well Crown ran its due diligence on junket operators, their owners or representatives, and the folks that they shuffled on and off an aeroplane to spray money around at the Australian casino sector. The Suncity junket was the subject of media allegations that stated that it was affiliated with The Company and that

Alvin Chau, the operator, was affiliated to the 14K triad. The Bergin report observed that Alvin Chau had been linked to triad activity over many years and there were suggestions that he held membership of the 14K Triad. This junket relationship was major to Crown and it was noted during the running of the Bergin inquiry that Alvin Chau was a key play in the junket scene in Macau and that Packer and senior crown management figures were keen to build a relationship with him because of the junket business he could bring to Crown. Packer, the inquiry report observed, kept a close eye on the Crown-Suncity relationship.

The relationship with Suncity was reviewed on 4 January 2017 given the problems that Crown had with arrests of Crown staff in China in October 2016. Additional reviews took place in March 2018 and March 2019 but no evidence was presented that would enlighten any external party as to why Crown continued to pursue its Suncity relationship. Dossiers on Chau were sought from various bodies that provided information on individuals globally. One of those dossiers from the Wealth-X firm was obtained in May 2016 and it said that Alvin Chau 'appears to have been a former member of the 14K Triad's Macau branch in the 1990s' and that Chau was reported to have handled loan sharking and gambling under the leadership of Kuok Koi Wan. Overseas media sources raised allegations that Alvin Chau had received stolen funds that were from the Bangladesh Central bank. Crown reviewed Alvin Chau's records held at the casino related to his risk rating. That review did not consider whether the junket operator that was alleged to have received stolen funds should continue to have junket operator status. Crown did review Alvin Chau's status as a money laundering risk in November 2018 and maintained his risk level as 'high' based on the information Crown had gathered, but the risk assessment also contained reflections on the media reportage that had been brought to Crown's attention over time. 'Crown Melbourne is aware of negative press on [Alvin Chau], including his potential links to Triads (as noted in ECDD conducted on him however notes that this commentary remains media speculation and that, to date, [Alvin Chau] has not been charged with an offence and has received his annual police clearance in Macau pursuant to the requirements of his DICJ (junket operator) license in that jurisdiction,' Crown's risk assessment observed. A further report on junket operators was commissioned by Crown from the Berkeley Research Group with further analysis on Alvin Chau. Crown had by reviewed the report dated 12 September 2020. It had arrived at a time when Crown had decided to pull the plug on engaging with junkets including Suncity.

Another junket operator also appeared in the Berkeley Research report with allegations of organised crime involvement. The Neptune Group Limited, which is listed on the Hong Kong Stock Exchange, was a junket operator with Crown since 2005 and there were reports of its former owner, Cheung Chi Tai, having links with the triads. His assets were also frozen in 2015 when he was linked to a $232 million money laundering venture involving the use of bank accounts in Hong Kong. That money laundering escapade prompted Crown to put stop codes on his customer account. Other operators within the Neptune Group were also involved with junkets with Crown and they also had allegations that related to links with organised crime and money laundering.

Another figure linked to junkets, Tom Zhou, was a part of what was known as the Chinatown Junket but he was more the money man rather than an actual operator of a junket. Zhou was described in media reports as being a man on the run with an Interpol red notice. He was also a premium player at Crown Perth and that lasted from February 2006 to February 2019. The casino decided it had enough of Tom Zhou because he had assaulted another patron and took action to stop him from coming into the venue. Crown faced a problem in the case of Tom Zhou as there were no adverse entries that appeared over the years. There were, however, allegations that emerged in July 2019 that he was wanted for money laundering and corruption. It was China that finally got their hands on him in January 2020 when he was arrested and extradited on money laundering and corruption allegations. Various other figures were linked to the Chinatown Junket but Bergin's report dismisses these characters as merely being 'front men'. Crown was unable to properly verify or conduct due diligence on the associated individuals and as such it was impossible for the casino to be able confirm that they were of 'good repute'.

Zehai Song was the head of the Song Junket, and he began running junkets with Crown from May 2009. He was seen as an important junket operator, but he also had an internal risk rating Crown designated as significant. Zehai Song was also an individual with whom Packer met in order to build a relationship with a junket operator that was perceived to be important. Crown got some information about Zehai Song and the due diligence report alleged that the junket operator was involved in illegal gambling and that he was convicted for gambling crimes for which he copped jail time back in 2003. 'Although Crown dealt with Zezhai Song as a Junket operator from 2009, it did not become aware of the reports that he had been charged with running an illegal gambling syndicate in China until it obtained the due diligence report in 2016,' the Bergin report observed. 'However it continued its relationship with Zezhai Song as the Song Junket operator until all its Junket operations were suspended in August 2020.'

Bergin report's findings on junkets

The Bergin inquiry took a deep dive into the junket operations and it was the foundational piece of investigation on which the Finkelstein royal commission would eventually build its own investigation and subsequent findings. What the Bergin report documents is that there were problems with the junket operations that were evident during the inquiry but that did not mean that Crown was—as alleged in media reports—linked to organised crime or that the company was 'wilfully blind or recklessly indifferent' to organised crime links. Crown cut ties with more than 100 junket operators linked to mainland China and it also acted fairly quickly in specific cases to ban or take other administrative action available to stop individuals such as Roy Moo and Tom Zhou from entering the premises. Bergin found that Crown was in most cases earnest in its efforts to do what it could to associate with clean junket operators but it was flawed. The media reportage of Crown being wilfully blind or recklessly indifferent to the existence of organised crime links was dismissed by Bergin.

What the inquiry and report handed by Bergin to the New South Wales regulator on matters concerning the junkets said what that there was one case study presented during the inquiry that merited deeper analysis and was of greater concern. The Suncity Junket and Alvin Chau case study pointed to the fact that there was information Crown had at its disposal to better understand what was going on with the Suncity junket. 'Clearly there were the obvious red flags of very large volumes of cash not under Crown's supervision in that room concurrently with publications that the Junket operator had links to organised crime groups,' Bergin's report observed. 'That concurrency should have alerted Crown to the obvious and urgent need to terminate its relationship with Suncity.' Crown management was described by Bergin as moving so slowing in considering the issues related to the Suncity Junket that any organised crime operatives would be relatively untroubled. This does not mean, Bergin asserted, that Crown's senior management were wilful or reckless when it came to evaluating the junket operators and attendees.

'Rather their consideration was flawed and in some respects rather befuddled,' Bergin's report said.

Imprisonment of Crown staff

Staff employed by Crown to promote the Crown business in China fell foul of the law for the promotion of gambling. The 19 staff embroiled in this saga were arrested in October 2016 in coordinated raids that would ultimately result in them being put on trial for breaching the Chinese criminal law. Their cases would be heard in June of the following year with all of the employees pleading guilty to a charge 'of assembling a crowd to engage in gambling'. The sentences imposed on 16 of the staff members involved fixed terms of imprisonment and fines. Five of the 16 staff copped 10 months imprisonment while 11 got nine months' imprisonment. Three administrative staff members did not receive any criminal penalty. It should be noted that the employees sentenced were not small fry—they were senior managers in Crown.

There were also South Korean staff that wound up being arrested for engaging in promotional activities. Legal advice was sought on 22 June 2015 and received the next day with law firm WilmerHale advising that charges involved the luring of Chinese to gamble in Korea and also the breach of laws or policies related to dealings in foreign currency. That advice noted that the 14 Korean employees were not China-based but had gone to promote gambling venues in China. There was also a need, the advice from WilmerHale said, to look at the arrests of Korean staff in the context of crackdowns on corruption. China had focused anti-corruption enforcement activities on Macau. Chinese gamblers wanted other places to go in order to avoid being sprung spraying their money in Macau. South Korea had turned into a location of choice. Further advice from WilmerHale obtained by Crown's operatives in the region explained how the law worked. The marketing efforts are clearly gambling. The marketing materials seized by the police show that the casinos offer free hotel, free air tickets, other free entertainment services to Chinese nationals so long as they gamble at the casinos, according to the legal advice cited in the Bergin report. 'These are the evidence used by the police department to prove that the marketing activities are illegal and the Korean casino representatives have been organising overseas gambling.' What WilmerHale also considered in its advice was the propensity for money laundering and foreign exchange evasion activities. There was a chain of activities that resulted in Chinese travel agencies that would receive money from gamblers wanting to go to a Korean casino. The money that is in the possession of the travel agents would then make its way to money laundering groups in China and then they would wind up with the Korean casino. The Chinese crackdown on money laundering and fancy foreign currency exchange games resulted in people desperate for a fancy flutter in a building with bright lights and strange sounds having to source secret electronic pipelines that would get the money they wanted out of China to finance their addiction. It is clear from other evidence and an extensive timeline of legal due diligence presented to the Bergin inquiry that there was always a constant risk that was eventually realised with Crown's employees being pressured to find new people to send to Crown venues overseas.

What ended up causing these arrests to occur? Media reports alleged that Crown knew its employees were breaking the law but counsel assisting the Bergin inquiry found no basis that Crown knew its staff were breaching Chinese laws. Crown did, nevertheless, expose its staff to what were risks of being quizzed by Chinese authorities given the nature of the work they were doing. The Bergin report brands Crown's behaviour as being 'reckless' where the promotion of Crown's venues was concerned. Interest from Chinese authorities, arrests of South

Korean employees, and the crackdown on foreign casinos and their operators were all factors that were known by Crown management, but they kept pushing for more sales. The Chinese crackdown on activities related to finding rich people with money to burn in overseas casinos was well known and Crown's own representatives tried to manage the behaviour of sales staff in order to ensure no 'overt' activity took place for a period of time while activity of law enforcement and regulators was at a peak. This was a clear indication that the operations were risky and that the staff were in harm's way simply by doing their job.

The board of directors of Crown were not entirely briefed about what was going on at various points in time in relation to the crackdown on international operations. Evidence was presented to the Bergin inquiry that pointed to the fact that materials intended for the boards of directors in terms of strategic business planning for the VIP International business went through several iterations. The crackdown announcement made by Chinese authorities was referred to in the drafts of a business plan covering the financial years between 2016 to 2020. It was in an earlier version or early versions of a draft. Something happened along the way. These documents might start full of detail, but they can gradually get trimmed and coiffed as they make their way through the process of being prettied up for the board of directors. Bergin refers to this process as the strategic plan being 'modified and abridged' and then 'further abridged' before landing on the desks or in the inboxes of members of the board of directors of Crown. Who was the genius that thought it was a bright idea to not tell the board that the Chinese authorities had announced a crackdown on the promotion of overseas gambling operations given that it was so fundamental for a board's understanding of business risks?

TAXING MOMENTS

Leaving aside whether the deductions were permissible, deliberately concealing the deductions from the regulator showed a tangible consciousness by those involved that what they were doing was wrong.

Adrian Finanzio, counsel assisting, The Royal Commission into the Casino Operator and Licence

Ms Halton said that she was shocked by what was reported in the article. Ms Korsanos and Mr Morrison said much the same thing. Mr Morrison said that everyone at the meeting was shocked by the magnitude of the potential underpayment.

The Report of the Royal Commission into the Casino Operator and Licence.

Decriminalising gambling and then taxing gambling revenue turned what was a vice into legitimate entertainment, and a source for government revenue. It would seem quite simple that this quid pro quo would be understood by anybody running a casino operation. Paying taxes to the government comes with the gig. It helps boost revenue as well as provide funds for the various research programs that exist to ensure that those who fall under the spell of the flashy and hypnotic gaming machines get some assistance to wean them off the gaming bug. Research done properly costs money and the responsible gambling foundations across Australia have plenty of it published or ongoing to assist governments and the community generally to understand the impact of gambling.

Paying taxes is an obligation that comes with the lucrative license to print money and in Victoria the obligation to put money into the government kitty sits in what is called the Management Agreement between Crown and the state government with 10 different amendments to the initial management agreement since it was first ratified by an Act of Parliament. The first management agreement was made between Crown and the state on 20 September 1993. These agreements set down the eyewatering amounts that a casino owner must pay to the government for the license as well as other taxes such as the tax on Gross Gambling Revenue. A pithy but useful operating definition of the gambling revenue amount in contention here was offered by counsel assisting: gross gambling revenue is the amount left over when amounts paid out as winnings to the lucky gamblers are deducted from the amount those very same gamblers fritter away on machines and tables games at the venue.

An obligation to pay taxation and keep one's nose clean would seem rather clear and obvious, but Crown played tricky games with tax compliance. Finkelstein noted that Crown showed a 'disregard of the law' by mucking about with a scheme aimed at minimising the amount of casino tax it would pay by claiming as tax deductions certain amounts that legal advisers said were not deductible or likely to not be deductible. Crown was forced to admit that it had attempted to hide the true substance of amounts it wanted to claim as deductions. The goal was to not get caught engaging in underpayment by the regulator. They got caught doing so by the royal commission and Finkelstein's report noted that more than $61 million had been paid by Crown in taxes and interest at the time the final report lobbed on desks.

The amount that was outstanding in casino taxes is in one sense irrelevant. Evidence presented before the royal commission provided an audit trail that demonstrates the willingness to dodge paying taxes owed to government. It does not matter whether the amount is five dollars or five thousand. The greater concern is the company had created a cultural mindset for tax minimisation that would lead it down a dead end.

What was the Crown tax scandal?

There was a point in time when Crown thought it could get away with trying to claim certain expenses as deductions to reduce the amount of tax it would pay to the government. Money that is earned comes through the door and certain amounts of cash spent to get that money through the door may be deductible. What Crown was trying to do was to find a way of fudging the classification of certain benefits to gamblers—the so-called gaming machine food program that consisted of meals that were given to gamblers when they spent a certain amount at the venue—so they would be regarded as a deductible expense and therefore minimising the amount on which tax was going to get paid. Those gaming machine meal program benefits formed a part of the eighth of eight different categories of promotional activities or loyalty programs that were examined closely during the royal commission. Other parts of that category included hotel accommodation and parking for gamblers. Seven other categories of loyalty programs existed, and they included pokie credit rewards, mail outs, jackpot payments, consolation, pokie credit tickets, and another pokie credit program called Matchplay. It was in 'Category 8' that Crown faced a particular challenge. The gambling giant had to assess what, if any, risk there was for the company's minimisation strategy to be detected by the regulator responsible for keeping Crown on the straight and narrow. This is again an example of Crown's management playing in a 'grey space' where everything seemed to be possible, allowable, and doable until somebody came along and waved a big finger in their face to say that it was not okay to play the game in this manner.

Take for example the messages shared within the ranks of senior management figures at Crown that were tabled during the hearings. One exhibit tabled sets out the objectives of the plan with a convenient quote from the late Kerry Packer during a parliamentary hearing in 1991 stating that 'If anyone in this country doesn't try to minimise their tax they want their heads read'. The proposal was to get a reclassification of what was known as the Gaming Machines Food Program in order to reduce gaming machines total revenue, reduce marketing costs, and reduce tax while also increasing gaming machines profit and the margin on the operation of the gaming machines. The road map for underpayment of tax was already in somebody's mind but what they needed was further advice on whether a regulator might notice the classification shuffle.

The revenue audit manager, Edwin Aquino, wrote in a 22 March 2012 memorandum in response to the proposals to reclassify the gaming machines food program to be a part of a bonus jackpot and labelled a gaming machine tax deduction that the proposed change would not be noticed by the regulator. Aquino said this view was arrived at after 'factoring in the refurbishment, economic environment, impacts from the negative publicity and the increase in gaming machines gaming tax by 1.72% in 1 July 2012'. The revenue audit manager suggested that there be a 'roll forward style explanation' in case the gambling regulator questioned the budgeted gambling tax when the paperwork was submitted to regulatory authorities. It was also noted that Crown's in-house counsel, Debra Tegoni, looked at the issue of classifying the food program as an amount paid out in winnings and she noted that the reclassification of the food program in a manner that would decrease the amount of tax payable was of low risk provided it did not alert anyone's interest. 'The risk may increase as and when more deductions are included over time,' Tegroni said in a 28 March 2022 memo. Finkelstein's report noted that this arrangement was not just meant to incorporate the food program. 'Crown Melbourne initially proposed to implement the deductions gradually, over a period of time,' Finkelstein said. 'This was a risk management strategy to conceal the deductions from the regulator.' The program was expanded slowly over the years by Crown's management so as to not arouse the regulator's suspicions.

Skimming from the top

Counsel assisting Finanzio was brutal in his assessment of the scheme as it was presented during the royal commission in his final address before Finkelstein took time out to draft the final report. The 2012 scheme was described by Finanzio as claiming deductions those expenses that were not winnings in order to reduce the payable gaming tax. It was in 2018—almost six years after the scheme began—that Crown began to fess up to reducing the amount on which they would ultimately pay tax. Evidence was tendered during the hearing about the way in which Crown began to gradually confess to some sins in the tax space. Finanzio said that Crown was 'too careful' in the way it approached making 'carefully honest disclosures'. Crown was branded by counsel assisting as not making the kind of full disclosures that are required of a suitable licensee. 'It did not make explicitly clear that the deductions were in relation to benefits that loyalty members were already entitled to by reason of their loyalty status,' the counsel assisting noted. 'In some instances, Crown was treating as a win the value of a benefit to which a member was entitled even before gambling commenced.'

Crown's chief executive officer at the relevant time in 2018, Xavier Walsh, said there was uncertainty about the classification being used but, according to counsel assisting, the only certainty was that here was no uncertainty about the status of the rebadging of certain member benefits as winnings. 'It was known at the time that the deductions for category eight when first commenced, that the activity was probably unlawful,' Finanzio said. 'Any uncertainty was put beyond doubt in October 2018. In its conduct with the [regulator], Crown was concerned to be able to say that it did not lie to the regulator, but Crown was happy that the regulator did not pick up on what was hiding in plain sight.'

It was in October 2018 that Crown had received legal advice that the practice of fudging what constituted the payment of winnings was unlawful. There was a period of time between October 2018 right up until the Finkelstein royal commission was due to commence that this fudging of gaming revenue to dodge paying tax remained a problem for Crown.

Telling the board about the tax dodge

The chair of Crown's board of directors, Helen Coonan, was first told in February 2021 about what were characterised as historical or legacy matters related to casino taxes by the Walsh. It was at the point that the royal commission had been called and Walsh had spoken about a legacy compliance issue. It was something Walsh did not go into great detail about with Coonan and that the then board chair has asked him to compile the necessary tax compliance paperwork for legal advice. Coonan was to consider this at some point, Walsh testified, and that he as chief executive officer would think about the best way to communicate these issues to the regulator. Coonan's evidence on the matter of her consideration of issues diverged with Walsh's during the public hearings. She was unsure of what Walsh meant by a note he made that was tendered to the royal commission. This difference, according to Finkelstein's report, was immaterial because, the royal commissioner said 'nothing turns on the different recollections'. The actual conversation on the topic was short and both Walsh and Coonan were the subject of analysis relating to what steps they could have taken to have been more particular about the issues involved in the casino tax non-compliance issues.

A spreadsheet with some rather ugly numbers on it was prepared following Walsh's conversation with Coonan. That spreadsheet covered the period between 2014 to 2019 and pointed to the fact that if all benefits paid out to gamblers in the form of Bonus Jackpots were not able to be deducted then the underpayment of casino tax was a whopping $167.8 million. The category of gambler benefits of which the food scheme was a part would represent an underpayment of $22.9 million. Walsh told the royal commission he was only concerned about the $22.9 million amount linked to the benefits that were a part of the gaming machine food program. Further meetings and discussions took place within Crown among senior managers responsible on these matters. It became clear that the board was not aware of the full extent of the non-compliance with the payment of casino taxes. Crown board member Jane Halton told the royal commission that she and other members of the Crown board were shocked by the news of the tax games being played within Crown. 'I can't tell you the exact words but I can tell you the—I mean, we could use a three-letter acronym,' Halton said. She told counsel assisting that the board members wanted to find out precisely what was going on with the casino tax matter as none of those present at a Risk Management Committee meeting when the news hit from the royal commission had no idea. This was in part because the board of directors had different people on it as Crown's governance structure was being overhauled. Other evidence from Halton also pointed to the fact that the full extent of the tax dilemma Crown had got itself into was not disclosed even when she met with management for discussions on those issues prior to the evidence being given by senior managers at the royal commission.

Crown ultimately agreed and acknowledged that there was underpayment of casino taxes and that it would review casino tax obligations from 2013 to 2021 in order to determine was it still owed to the state government with any adjustments made for the goods and services tax. Crown stopped the tax deduction rort on what it called Category 8 promotions and there were promotions that formed a part of another category that Crown said it would no longer run. Finkelstein also noted that there was also another likely casino tax underpayment problem for Crown that needed further examination.

Crown announcement released

Crown Casino had to front the market with the news of non-compliance with its agreements to pay an agreed amount of tax to the state government once the royal commission had aired the underpayments. There was a market release sent through the Australian Securities Exchange that outlined the fact that it had sinned and was doing penance. 'Crown has resolved to make a payment to the Victorian Commission for Gambling and Liquor Regulation representing an underpayment of casino tax by Crown Melbourne of approximately $37 million over the period commencing in the 2012 financial year to date relating to the incorrect deduction of certain bonus rewards provided to patrons in connection with play on Crown Melbourne's electronic gaming machines,' the casino's announcement said.

There is another little thing Crown noted in its market update. It wasn't just the $37 million that Crown had to cough up for trying to be tricky and dodge paying taxes. There was an interest payment as well that Crown was obliged to pay that hit $24 million. This interest payment and the and the $37 million make up the $61 million amount that the casino bossed had to make sure was paid to the state government in order to square the ledger. Paying that amount back in taxes was not the only bit of homework Crown's board of directors, senior managers and members had on their collective plate. 'Crown is continuing its review of other aspects of casino tax payments and will update the market once the review is complete,' the announcement said. 'Crown's review includes a review of Matchplay, the loyalty promotion pursuant to which Crown Rewards Points are redeemed for credits for use in electronic gaming machines.' The regulator had also advised Crown that the commission's final report would give rise to the regulator finalising what it believed was Crown's final tax obligation to the state.

FREE GROG, FISHING TRIPS, MARRIAGES AND KEEPING YOURSELF NICE

The independence and objectivity of the regulator in the performance of its function is an important contributor to its effectiveness and the maintenance of the public's trust and confidence in the regulator.

Perth Casino Royal Commission Final Report, March 2022

The emails passing between Connolly, Preston, Hulme and Marais lacked the professionalism, objectivity and requisite degree of formality of an appropriate regulatory posture.

Perth Casino Royal Commission Final Report, March 2022

The Perth Casino Royal Commission took the findings of the other two inquiries and then built on them with a report of almost 1000 pages in length that not only gave Crown's operations an evisceration in a similar fashion as the Bergin and Finkelstein inquiries. It explored the notions of conflicts of interest and the adequacy of government codes of conduct in the context of regulating the sole casino in the state. A code of conduct existed, the report from the inquiry mounted in the West acknowledged, but there was a need to put more muscle on a skeleton given case studies presented to the commission that constituted conflicts of interest appeared to suggest that the principles the document laid out needed further clarity. Multiple examples of relationships between staff working for a department or a regulator and people working for the regulated entity were peppered throughout the inquiry and those examples prompted suggested revisions to a code of conduct that the royal commission believed was a bit light on.

Gambling not on, but what else is ruled out?

It should be observed at the outset that the Code of Conduct made quite clear that gambling at the venue that somebody is employed to regulate is not permitted under the Code of Conduct. That is not okay. It is clear in the words that it is not something a person involved in casino regulation should be doing, but the royal commissioners hearing evidence in a courtroom in Perth were not satisfied that the Code said enough given the numerous perceived conflicts that existed. The section on conflicts, according to the Perth Casino report, needed additional material to set down other possible ways in which people may be compromised or could be considered by a third party to be compromised in their role as a regulator. What exactly did they mean?

Gaming is an understandable prohibition and one that is clear but there are other facilities at the Perth Casino complex. The royal commissioners in Perth noted that it might not be advisable to stay in accommodation at the Crown Perth Resort because that risks room upgrades and free grog being provided to any person that is identified as working with the regulator. This recommendation for a code of conduct upgrade did not emerge by accident. Evidence was presented to the royal commission that management in the department used to have a practice of taking senior staff to an eatery at the Perth Crown Resort for Christmas. They would have their end of year Christmas lunch there. Resort management would saunter over, visit the department's team, and see whether they were enjoying the hospitality. There was even a complimentary bottle of grog sent over to the table one year.

Regulators should never allow themselves to be seen as if they are on the take or would give preference to an entity when enforcing rules, and these kinds of practices would create the perception that the regulator would be persuaded to adopt the view of the entity to be regulated. There was also detail absent in relation to who can give or accept gifts and benefits in their role as a regulator of a casino that the final report. It was clear from evidence and the absence of more detailed guidance that people needed more detail. Disclosure of attendance at social events that may be held at Crown Perth is also an issue that was raised.

These issues were brought up by the royal commissioners because it became clear during the course of the examination of the Perth Casino's activities and the manner in which they were regulated that processes designed to protect the regulator from criticism and perceptions of conflict.

Personal relationships

Multiple cases of different relationships that existed between people that worked in regulatory roles and those that worked at Crown Perth Resorts raised questions about the way in which the management in the regulatory apparatus managed potential conflicts. The royal commission found that this was not a strong point for those in the regulatory function and that the code of conduct needed additional material to make consideration of relationships more robust. 'Personal relationships between officers of the regulator and officers of the licensee, if not properly managed, have the potential to compromise the regulator's objectivity and independence and the public's perception of the same,' the report said. 'The [Code of Conduct] does not explicitly identify how personal relationships give rise to conflicts of interest and how such conflicts should be managed.' This suggestion from the royal commissioners comes after pages upon pages of revelations of issues with relationships that could pose a threat to the perception of regulatory independence.

One case study concerned Officer A, a former employee of the department and he carried out inspections at the Perth Casino for two decades. Officer A said that the approach to conflicts morphed over time because attitudes appeared to change. 'They recalled that when they first started work it was clear that inspectors could not have any relationship with casino employees outside of work, but that policy relaxed over time to the point that relationships were not prohibited,' the report says. 'They said there was no formal policy change, rather an observed change in attitude, concluded by how the Department reacted to those relationships.' Officer A married a Perth Casino employee who was a table games inspector and the marriage occurred while Officer A was still a departmental inspector. The relationship was disclosed of Officer A's supervisors. They managed the conflict of interest by ensuring that they did not conduct audits of groups of tables or the pit where ethe spouse worked and by not being involved in any audit that might include their spouse. The report notes that Officer A was promoted to the role of senior inspector and that the new role did not require them to deal with their spouse on work-related matters. Officer A told the royal commission that they accepted it would have been more appropriate for the two of them to not be involved in casino regulation at all.

Another officer known as Officer B in the report and they were employed by the department regulating the casino since 1990. Various roles were held by Officer B and this included become a senior compliance inspector. There was a family member that worked as a croupier at the casino for six years while Officer B was an inspector and senior inspector. Officer B's colleagues and relevant managers were available of the family member's employment but it was not subject to formal recording in a system. Officer B said various inspectors had family working at the casino at that specific time with no guidance being given on how best to manage the conflicts as they arose. No regulatory investigation or audit was performed by Officer B that involved the work of their family member nor was there any instructions given by Officer B to any investigator they supervised to not audit or investigate work done by the member of their family.

Fishing trip buddies

There was also the group that spent time going on fishing trips on weekends. They used work emails to tee up their trips and went out to throw their lines and sinkers out for kicks. What interested the royal commission was this group was made up of somebody working for the regulator and people working for the regulated. The key witness at the inquiry on this particular issue was Michael Connolly. Connolly was the chief casino officer with the responsibility of being the regulator's key player in dealing with the submissions made by the Perth Casino to the regulator. This was a key position of influence and there were decisions he was able to make in relation to casino regulation. Paul Hulme, Jon Nichols and Claude Marais were all friends of Connolly's. Hulme worked with Connolly in the public service but later went to work at Crown Perth as one of their Legal and compliance team. Both have stayed in touch over the year. Nichols was also a public servant and met Connolly at the department before working at Crown. Nichols was not somebody in charge of operations at the casino while employed at Crown. Marais worked at Crown Perth when he first met Connolly in 2012 and Connolly had an understanding that Marais was responsible for all Crown's compliance obligations. Marais liked fishing. Connolly liked fishing. They went out on fishing trips several times in the years that followed. There is one other relationship that needs coverage here and that is the one with Joshua Preston who was known to Connolly as being the Chie Legal officer of Perth Casino.

Connolly took Marais out on fishing trips on a periodic basis. The royal commissioner heard that Connolly and Marais went for annual crayfish expeditions with the exception of 2019 and there were trips that involved the other Crown employees mentioned above. Connolly used his department e-mail and Marais, Hulme and Preston used their Crown emails to talk about fishing boats and other matters that were addressed informally. The royal commissioners said that the emails were 'not suited to the maintenance of a professional relationship and the respect which the officers of the casino ought to have for the CCO'. A paragraph on the emails circulated by the Crown heavyweights and their fishing companion later in the report describes them as being written in 'familiar jocular tone and expressed "blokeish" sentiments or themes'. These email exchanges seem to go on even when there was serious regulatory business to discuss. 'For example, in 2014, the [regulator] instructed Connolly to liaise with Perth Casino with a view to changing the minimum speed of an EGM game from five seconds to six seconds (that is, to slow the game down),' the report said. 'At the same time, Connolly was emailing Preston, Hulme and Marais about boating and fishing.' It was accepted by Connolly that emailing people about extracurricular activities when there was actually a serious issue about slowing the pace of electronic games on the table for resolution.

The Perth Casino inquiry's report details a range of interactions between the legal and compliance team from Crown and Connolly in his regulatory capacity. The conclusions that the Crown Perth inquisitors ultimately came to was that the friendship between Nichols and Connolly needed declaration to the department and then consequently that declaration needed to be provided to the casino regulator. No evidence was provided to the committee that a notification took place. The evidence before the committee was that Nicholls had no significant role in operations at the Perth Casino and that any declaration would not have resulted in the need to manage that one. The other relationships are just a little different. Hulme and Marais were key legal officers at the Crown Perth and they were both professionally involved in dealing with Connolly on regulatory matters. There were clear conflicts in these situations and declarations should have been made and the department should have managed them.

What did they find in relation to the impact of these relationships? There were three factors highlighted in the report. It was likely, according to the royal commissioners, that Connolly's objectivity was compromised when carry out his role as regulator, the friendships placed him in a position of conflict between his duties in the public interest regarding regulation and his personal friendships, and the friendships would create a perception in the minds of the public that the department and regulator may have been unduly influenced by the relationships or provided preferential treatment to the casino. 'The PCRC reaches this conclusion, notwithstanding Connolly's evidence that his friendships with Crown employees had not influenced any decision he had made,' the royal commissioners said. 'A person may believe that they are acting in the best interests of a party to whom they owe a public duty (here, the regulator, GWC) but their objectivity and judgement may nevertheless be affected by a conflict of interest.'

UNEASY STALEMATE

The Government accepts all of the findings of the Royal Commission and we are taking immediate action to hold Crown to account and restore the public's trust in the casino operator.

Melissa Horne, Minister for Consumer Affairs, Gaming and Liquor Regulation

Crown will work constructively and cooperatively with the Victorian Government in relation to the findings and recommendations of the Report and their response.

Crown Resorts Limited Media Release

If… the regulator is not 'clearly satisfied' that Crown Melbourne is suitable to hold its casino licence, the licence will be cancelled forthwith.

Ray Finkelstein, Royal Commissioner

The late Rushworth, or Rush, Kidder, was an ethicist and journalist who had written and spoken extensively about the challenges of making ethical decisions. Kidder, who died in 2012 aged 67, began as a journalist who devoted a life to studying ethics. He wrote a book called *How good people make tough choices*, an examination of how tough decisions need to be made. What Kidder outlined was the fact that the difference between right and wrong or good and bad is simple. Nothing about that scenario is hard. What is tougher, Kidder argued, was the difference between right and right. There are times when an ethical decision will end up being a choice between two or more options that could be equally 'right'—whatever right happens to mean at a point in time and within the context of a situation. Kidder was also someone who looked at decisions through the filter of something being just—the delivery of justice or a just outcome—and being merciful. Delivering a decision that acknowledges a transgression but that there a sense of mercy about the situation.

Kidder's general logic can be applied when considering the way in which the heads of the respective inquiries—Finkelstein, Bergin and Owen—were challenged when they were grappling with the way in which to address the issue of fitness of the corporation to hold a license and what that same corporation that was found wanting in some many different ways needed to do to rehabilitate itself to keep the license or licenses it had that were in essence bits of paper letting these companies sitting under Crown Resorts to print money.

Key considerations in decision making

What would be the right decision in circumstances where a corporate entity had failed to meet community standards and expectations? Finkelstein's report provides some insight into precisely what factors a royal commissioner needs to take into account when considering recommendations. Among the issues was the fact that sin binning Crown was justified. There is a laundry list of reasons why cancellation of the casino license could have taken place and it is understandable why people would argue for cancellation on the basis of this list alone irrespective of any other consideration. The factors at the heart of this included the fact crooks were gambling in the casino, money laundering took place, taxes went unpaid, Chinese high worth gamblers were being assisted to shuffle money out of their country to a value of

$160 million, the regulator was bullied and investigators were misled, the safety of employees was risked and certain employees were jailed, some staff were encouraged to commit fraud by falsifying documents, and there were gamblers that were encouraged to let Crown empty the contents of their bank accounts and wallets as they gambled their funds away. The issue here is culture and throughout the royal commission it was apparent that there were senior executives that encouraged conduct that resulted in risks being taken that were unacceptable. This is not new, novel or exclusive to the gambling enterprises run by Crown. Any examination of companies that collapse will usually point to a failure of corporate culture. Culture is determined by people and Finkelstein hits some of those folks between the eyeballs with a blunt assessment of their conduct. 'Senior executives also were plainly at fault. They were responsible for the day-to-day affairs of the organisation,' Finkelstein said. 'It was their job to make sure that all legal and regulatory obligations were, in fact, satisfied.' It is observed in the report that many senior executives were responsible for wrongdoing regardless of whether they authorised bad behaviour or simply suspected it and took the matter no further. 'It is open to conclude that the actions of certain senior executives were so unsatisfactory that they should no longer have any role in the affairs of a public company,' the Finkelstein report said.

One of the key reasons for misconduct highlighted throughout the royal commission was the pursuit of profit. The royal commissioner was unconvinced that the cultural problem is simply explained by people who were given the responsibility to chase profits. That was deemed too easy an answer on its own and something else lurked in the back of the minds of senior executives and their legal counsel. The reality of being an enterprise that was taking operation risks of this type was that it would ultimately lead to confrontations with regulatory authorities. Finkelstein noted that there was—to coin a euphemism—an unhealthy compliance culture in the Crown stable of enterprises and this meant that people were focused on, firstly, what the chances were of getting caught and, secondly, how much it was likely to cost the corporation. Gambling—in other words—did not just take place on the tables in the main floor of the casino. It was intrinsic to the culture of how parts of the organisation were run. 'Many senior executives adopted this mindset. Their decision whether or not to engage in improper, or probably improper, conduct was made by considering the chance of discovery and sanction,' Finkelstein said. 'If these executives thought Crown Melbourne would get away with improper conduct that was otherwise beneficial, they did not hesitate in going ahead. It was only when conduct was plainly unlawful that it was rejected.' Playing chase with the regulators and attempting to avoid being pinged for breaches was not solely the province of the executives.

Legal minds were caught up in the game of cat and mouse as well and Finkelstein does not spare the legal profession from a tongue lashing. External and internal legal advisers were just as much a part of playing cat and mouse with regulatory authorities. 'There were occasions when Crown Melbourne was investigated by the regulator. Some investigations concerned alleged wrongdoing,' Finkelstein observed. 'Strategies were adopted to thwart and frustrate the regulatory process. All too often, these strategies were devised by lawyers or, at least, they were willing accomplices.' The royal commissioner echoed sentiments made by other royal commissioners such as Neville Owen that looked at similar egregious failures in corporate governance. 'At no point did any lawyer say, "This is improper" or "A regulated entity must always remain suitable, and consistent with the privilege it has been given, should not engage in this type of conduct",' Finkelstein said. One legal mind appearing before the royal commission said they thought it was not their role to be telling the client what they should or should not be doing. Finkelstein hit hard. He did not miss. 'Put more directly, rather than a lawyer simply advising a client whether a given course of action is completely legal, in an appropriate case (and whether the case is appropriate will usually be self-evident) the lawyer could ask their client of the proposed conduct: "Is it right?", "Is it honest?" and "Does it thwart the purpose of the law?",' the royal commissioner said. He added that moral advice could be given by lawyers in a context where it is not an imposition but that it flags matters worthy of consideration that could help people avoid walking down the darker end of the street.

The rot that had set in at Crown provided a compelling case for an argument that the license should be cancelled but there were a range of other considerations that needed to be factored into the equation. Crown has begun a program of reforming its processes and it had seen a gradual turnover of members of the board of directors and senior management. Corporate culture is created by people and the fact individuals had moved on from the gambling giant was an indication that there was a chance of rehabilitation. Crown itself had written to the state government in the form of a pre-emptive strike for the state government to ignore any recommendation to cancel the license because it had expressed concern that it would lead to defaults in financing agreements. The dominoes would fall, according to Crown, because any default on financial matters had the potential to impact on all stakeholders such as shareholders and employees, cause the loss of 11,000 jobs, and attract overseas buyers that might just want to get their hands on a glittering prize they would regard as a renovator's dream. Crown argued in its letter to the state government that the possible financial apocalypse for Crown and the potential aftereffects meant that it was not in the public interest for Crown to lose its license. This letter was referred to in the final report by Finkelstein because Crown had bypassed the royal commissioner and sought to get its view on how operations should be regulated after the commission to the government before the Fink's final report. 'The purpose of the letter was to persuade the Minister not to accept any recommendation by the Commission that Crown Melbourne's casino licence be cancelled or suspended,' Finkelstein observed. 'Not surprisingly, Crown directors' lawyers did not provide a copy of the letter to the Commission. Quite properly, the State's solicitors did.'

Finkelstein's report delves into multiple threads that are or should be considered in reaching a final view on what should happen with Crown. The contribution of Crown to a state that is a prized tourist destination is acknowledged as is the flow on benefit the complex on Southbank provides to other businesses such as restaurants, cinemas, and gift shops. The more important consideration, however, for Finkelstein is the issue related to what the casino's board of directors and senior management need to take to get the venue back to suitability. There is also the question of whether there is a better way of dealing with Finkelstein's rap sheet of misdemeanours littered throughout the report other than pulling the rug from under Crown completely by rescinding the license. Avoiding a range of harms that would come from cancelling the license was clearly on his mind and this was not just because of Crown's forecast of an economic apocalypse in that letter sent to the state government. Finkelstein also pointed to dire consequences that could flow from license cancellation. This meant coming up with an answer that minimised greater harm but also provided an incentive for the organisation to rehabilitate itself.

Crown deemed unsuitable

Both the Bergin and Finkelstein endeavours found that the behemoth that is Crown was guilty of a string of sins that at the time of both inquiries concluding the gambling giant was deemed unfit to hold licenses and the inquiry in Western Australia was still going through its motions hearing evidence as 2021 can to a close. There was no such thing as a company secret on the material issues of concern for Crown any longer because the inquiries had kicked that door open. This was a corporate titan that had its innards stripped open, spread across inquiry tables, and the key details reported on by print, radio and television. The Bergin and Finkelstein reviews resulted in Crown having to get used to external monitors or observers sitting right behind it and looking over its shoulder at every single move if it wanted to continue to participate in the gambling business in Australia.

The NSW independent monitor

The Bergin Inquiry report was released in February 2021 but there were follow up media releases from the Liquor and Gaming Authority, which instigated the inquiry into Crown, that indicated that there was scope for Crown to get back to some form of fitness—a fitness program if you will—in order to be considered suitable to hold a license to run the Barangaroo complex. A media release from the Independent Liquor and Gaming Authority issued in May 2021 reported that Crown had agreed to pay a proportion of the costs of the public inquiry into their operations that the company stated in a separate release would cost it $12.5 million. Crown also agreed, according to the regulator, to begin paying the Casino Supervisory Levy of $5 million for both 2021 and 2022. Crown had flagged it would stop dealing with junket operators but it had also agreed with the regulator to ensure this remained the case.

Crown had also said it would investigate the options for the introduction of cashless gaming cards at Crown Sydney. Then executive chairman at the time, Helen Coonan, said in Crown's release to the market issued in response to the liquor and gaming regulator's announcement that the company recognised there was more work left to do in Crown. 'It's important to know we are well on track but I have assured the regulator there will be no complacency as we continue to embed the changes to improve our governance and compliance processes across the organisation,' Coonan said.

The liquor and gaming supremo's media release also flagged that Crown was busily trying to rehabilitate its reputation with the regulator by making significant internal changes. Changes in the batting line up of the board of directors and senior management were noted as having taken place and that senior executive positions were filled by people with relevant expertise and experience. The fact that Crown was getting independent audits completed on various parts of its operations to satisfy the authority that it was getting itself to a stage where it could be considered fit to hold a license is also mentioned with Crawford noting that Crown was cooperating with the regulator in addressing the concerns raised in the Bergin probe. Consolidated Press Holdings had also agreed to address issues of control and influence over the high roller's gambling den.

There is an independent monitor that was to be appointed at the time of the media release's issue in order to observe and report back to the regulator on structural changes in order to help the regulator decide whether Crown could morph itself into an entity that meets the suitability criteria. Three prominent areas were a part of the independent monitor's brief: corporate governance, money laundering, and culture—areas that were to be addressed extensively in Volume Two of Bergin's report. 'The Authority will await the report from the Independent Monitor, and the result of the financial accounts audit, before making a final decision on suitability,' Crawford said. 'Any changes to Crown's ownership structure, including takeover or merger proposals, require the Authority to consider a range of issues including undertaking full probity assessments of any new entrants, how a merged entity would operate, and the extent to which any existing agreements with Crown would need to be reviewed.'

This does not mean that the regulator was above giving Crown some assistance to keep parts of the Sydney operation kicking along while it dealt with the issues arising from the review by Bergin. Non-gaming areas at the Barangaroo resort needed the renewal of interim liquor licenses in October 2021 and this was done again as an interim measure. Crown and the regulator had come to an agreement in December 2020 that non-gaming parts of the complex would be able to serve alcohol. This included accommodation, restaurants, entertainment and other areas in the complex that had bars for patrons. 'ILGA's position on Crown Sydney's gaming operations has not changed, with the Authority still monitoring and assessing Crown's responses to the issues arising from the Bergin Report,' Crawford said. 'These issues are complex, and Crown is required to undertake significant change to satisfy the Authority that it is on a pathway to become suitable to hold a gaming licence. It will take further time for Crown to fully implement that change and for the Authority to give it proper consideration before making its determination.' The regulator also updated its web site in October and December 2021 with fresh orders that approved amended rules for six games to be played at the Crown Sydney restricted gaming complex.

It took the New South Wales government until August to formally respond to the Bergin Report in order to strengthen aspects of its gambling legislation with Victor Dominello, the Minister for Digital and Customer Service in New South Wales, stating in an 18 August 2021 media release that the government will support all of the recommendations from the Bergin Report on the regulation of casinos as well as recommendations on the suitability of Crown Resorts to hold a restricted gaming license. Dominello said that the government was committed to establishing an independent casino regulator as well as making legislative reforms that were focused on by Bergin. 'The NSW Government response to the Bergin Inquiry will see a redesigned regulatory structure for casinos in NSW, with a clearer focus on addressing money laundering risks inherently associated with casino activities,' Dominello said. 'It is critical the management and operation of casinos in NSW are free from criminal influence and exploitation. Committing to implement the 19 recommendations from Justice Bergin's report is an important first step in the process of reforming the casino sector.' A new regulator for casinos, according to Dominello, would be funded by a casino supervisory levy.

This new regulatory body would not just be any kind of bureaucracy. Bergin stipulated that an independent casino commission should have powers equivalent to that of a royal commission, and it should be a specialist regulator presided over by people that would understand the complexities of the running of a gambling enterprise such as a casino. 'It should not be distracted by obligations pertaining to matters outside the regulated casinos in New South Wales and should focus only on the objects of the Casino Control Act,' she wrote. 'Having regard to what has been observed in respect of the inefficiencies in the present bifurcated structure it would be counter-productive to burden the ICC with the general regulation of clubs, pubs, non-casino gaming and liquor licensing problems.' Bergin points to the regulatory structures in Singapore as well as Massachusetts as examples of places that provide guidance to governments in Australia.

It was intended by Bergin that the independent casino commission, which is to be funded from contributions from the gambling sector as a part of a 'user pays' approach to regulation, would be the organisation that that would be solely responsible for making decisions about an entity licensed to run casinos and this included what, if any, disciplinary action was appropriate against a licensee. This underscores a critical issue when it comes to regulation of a sector that can draw criminal elements close to it in the same way as a summer barbeque in Australia draws blowflies. The commission could not under this model shift blame or flick the responsibility to another agency or agencies. It would have to decide on the appropriateness or otherwise of a casino's conduct of its own accord.

The new regime as envisaged by Bergin would require any holder of a casino license to ensure they engaged and independent and appropriately qualified auditor to look at a casino's compliance with all relevant legislation. A compliance auditor would be required to report to the casino commission on an annual basis on whether an entity has complied with all of its obligations. The recommendations from Bergin would require the compliance auditor to report to both the casino and the casino commission at the same time if it found suspicious activities putting compliance with rules at risk or a contravention of laws or regulations had occurred or will occur. This is fine for casino-related matters that can easily be dealt with under State legislation. Listed companies dealt with federal, state and local government laws, regulations, and by-laws each day and negotiating the jurisdictional boundaries was clearly on Bergin's mind as she drafted her report and contemplated the form a new regulator or commission may take and what, if any, interaction that commission should have with other parts of the legislative and law enforcement framework. Bergin calls for the consideration of giving the independent casino commission the ability to refer information to bodies such as the Australian Securities and Investments Commission. The corporate regulator has both the responsibility and the ability to enforce company laws in Australia and any investigations of an entity that runs a casino by an independent casino commission might necessitate an investigation and possibly enforcement action. Enabling information sharing between regulatory and enforcement agencies across jurisdictions means that offences that can be investigated and prosecuted by Commonwealth authorities is made easier.

Bergin's report had a laser-like focus on the big picture issues of concern and the prescription to treat some of the ills are functioned as a precursor to what was to come when the royal commission spearheaded by Finkelstein was to report. The New South Wales liquor and gaming regulator's continuing conversations with Crown Resorts on how best to rehabilitate its operations were ongoing while Finkelstein's inquiry was running. The use of an independent monitor to report back on Crown's progress to meeting suitability to the regulator in New South Wales was a model that would emerge in another way in Victoria.

A babysitter for Crown

Finkelstein's report found that Crown was unfit to hold the casino license because of all of the breaches of law and transgressions that were played out before the royal commissioner and his legal team. That finding was unsurprising. It mirrored the eviscerating Bergin report that tore into Crown's governance, internal controls, dalliances with organised crime, and breaches of gaming rules that had not only been recorded as evidence during the Bergin inquiry but replicated in the work done by Finkelstein. The chief inquirer said in the report that there was a major dilemma that faced him when contemplating what to recommended in the context of a business that had engaged in conduct described in the report as 'disgraceful'. 'Deciding what to recommend was a demanding task. It required the weighing up of two almost irreconcilable positions. On one side, there was the overriding need to maintain the integrity of the licensing system. That requires the cancellation of a casino licence held by an unsuitable person,' Finkelstein said. 'On the other side, there were two factors: the risk that cancellation of Crown Melbourne's licence would cause considerable harm to the Victorian economy and innocent third parties; and whether, in a short time, Crown Melbourne could so 'remake' itself that it would once again become suitable to hold a casino licence.' The royal commissioner acknowledged that criticisms were bound to head in his direction regardless of the direction he decided to pursue in the case of Crown given the prominence of the transgressions as well as the prominence of the role Crown plays in the Victorian economy. Crown was in many respects much like the banking sector that was kicked about during the Hayne Royal Commission: too big to fail.

The report into Crown's travails in and out of strife acknowledged that there were already major changes that had taken place and that Crown's changes to management, processes and procedures was a key factor in there being no recommendation that the license currently held be revoked. 'Although Crown Melbourne rightly deserves criticism for its past misconduct, and no one connected with the organisation is entitled to much sympathy, what tipped the balance against the cancellation of its licence was that Crown Melbourne has, at great financial cost, embarked on a significant reform program led by people of good will and skill,' Finkelstein said. 'The program is likely to succeed. If it does, that will be to the benefit of Victoria.' There was a clean out of personnel that is hardly a novel move given that companies that hit strife tend to try resuscitating a business with a new set of hands on the steering wheel. Changes in the membership of the board of directors provided Finkelstein with an opportunity to both acknowledge the evidence that changes were progressing but to also set a two-year time frame during which Crown must demonstrate an improved state of governance or they would be waving the license goodbye.

Finkelstein threw the management and board of directors a lifeline by creating a kind of public interest guardian angel—a special manager to look over the shoulder of the Crown Casino board and management. This is an addition to the enhanced monitoring that will be in place if Crown Sydney meets the requirements of the New South Wales regulator and the independent monitor. The special manager's role is meant to function as an accountability mechanism to ensure Crown was behaving itself. 'This manager, most likely a firm, will oversee all aspects of the casino's operations. It will keep a watchful eye on the progress of reform,' the report said. 'It will make sure that all rules and regulations are complied with. It will investigate particular aspects of the casino's operations.' Finkelstein was adamant that there should be no more inquiries into Crown when the two-year period concludes. The reviews into Crown by authorities in New South Wales, Victoria and Western Australia, Finkelstein argued, and any special manager's report should be enough alongside those previous deep dives for the regulator to come to a view on whether Crown should continue to run a gambling and gaming business.

The Victorian Government announced on 26 October 2021 that it welcomed the Finkelstein recommendations and that it would move to institute nine of the 33 recommendations made in the final report. One of those was to herald the appointment Stephen O'Bryan QC, a former chairman of the Independent Broad-Based Anti-Corruption Commission, to the role of the special manager. The minister responsible for the gaming sector, Melissa Horne, told the Victorian Parliament when introducing the Casino and Gambling Legislation Amendment Bill 2021, which also creates the Victorian Gambling and Casino Control Commission, about the extraordinary power with which O'Bryan has as a special manager of the casino will be granted under law including the fact that the special manager has the capacity to tell the board of the casino what actions it can and cannot take in specific circumstances and that the special manager will be able to get resources to ensure he can do his job properly. The law specifies that the special manager 'has full and free access to all the books and records' of Crown Resorts and that the special manager has all the powers, rights and privileges of a member of the Board of Directors. The special manager will also be able to attend any meeting of the board of directors or a committee of the board in order to fulfill the obligations under law to report to the regulator on Crown's progress. 'The Government and the regulator will be kept informed; the Special Manager will provide formal reports to government and the regulator every six months on Crown's remediation efforts,' the Minister said. 'The Special Manager's final report will make a recommendation to the regulator regarding Crown's suitability to hold its licence. The regulator must be "clearly satisfied" that Crown Melbourne has reached suitability.'

Greater scrutiny and larger fines

The explanatory memorandum to the legislation as debated in parliament set out the increase in fines and the expanded disciplinary regime that would apply to casinos and those that operate them should they veer should they cross the new regulator for gambling and casinos. A maximum fine of $100 million could be levelled at a casino. 'The increase in the maximum fine follows recommendations of the Royal Commission and the independent policy review which found that the penalties under the Act are wholly inadequate and not proportionate to the risks and harm associated with casino operations,' the explanatory memorandum said. Changing the total cost of a fine also means that what might previously have been considered by a casino operator as a mere cost of doing business such as a tax becomes more costly. Doing the wrong thing would create a greater dent in the company's bottom line and costing the ultimate owners, the shareholders, more.

There were also new grounds for disciplinary action put into the legislation such as the failure of the casino operator to implement a recommendation of the new commission created under law. The Bill empowered the commission to tell the casino operator what it can and cannot do after there has been an investigation into an issue brought to the attention of the casino regulator. The legislation prohibits gambling junkets that were a part of the cause of imported problems, and it also embeds a definition of 'maladministration' that is certain to heighten tensions around the board table and in the offices of senior managers at Crown Resorts. Maladministration, according to the amendments made to the Casino Control Act 1991, encompasses conduct that is either based in whole or part on improper motives conduct that is unreasonable, unjust, or oppressive and—just for good measure—conduct that is negligent.

Where to from here?

Giving large businesses a second chance when they have been riddled with problems may not satisfy the observer that wants pure justice delivered and wrongdoers penalised in the strongest way possible. That perspective is often cloaked in anger and understandable righteousness when holders of the precious commodity such as a casino license is guilty of numerous cases of misbehaviour. Crown certainly gave the regulators, the royal commissioner Victoria and the chair of the inquiry in New South Wales enough cause to throw the thickest book with the hardest of covers at them not just once but multiple times. The question posed by Kidder all those years ago about how you determine the action that is most right in the circumstances where there are several possible outcomes that could be justified is the one that clearly perplexed both

Bergin and Finkelstein. That answer is never arrived at easily and nor is it meant to be easy. It requires every ounce of experience and a sprinkling of the wisdom of Solomon to ensure that a desired outcome is reached without causing greater harm to a community that had along with the rest of the world suffered throughout a pandemic. Will giving people time to clean house and put new processes and procedures in place result in a gambling establishment with less interaction with organised crime elements and fewer gamblers being exploited for profit? No politician, author, regulator or general punter from the public is able to determine that ahead of time. The running of a gambling enterprise and the gambling and wagering sector more generally should be seen in the same light as a piece of complex machinery or a clock. Every gear needs to be working well, oiled when required, and subject to maintenance and inspection when regulations or manuals state these must take place. Organisations can become poorly run when systems and processes—external and internal—are allowed to decay as they were so clearly in the case of Crown. The organisation has been given the chance to redeem itself within a timeframe and regulators have been given a new lick of paint and a more specific remit to get back to regulating properly. Only time will tell whether all of these changes improve the culture of an organisation that has been suffering because of games played in the shadows by people who should not have required a royal commission to remind them that they were in a position of power and in possession of the necessary knowledge and intellectual capacity to know better.

ACKNOWLEDGEMENTS

This is the third book I have written for Wilkinson Publishing that looks at the way in which businesses and individuals exploit the vulnerable for their own advantage and tackled different aspects of regulation related to people getting compensation. *Vulture City* was about the Hayne Royal Commission and the litany of examples heard by Kenneth Hayne and his top flight legal team about the behaviour of a corporate culture that placed profit above the consumer. *Rorts and Rip-Offs* was the flipside of *Vulture City*—that book was written to empower consumers to ask questions before they click a button to purchase goods online, pay somebody for financial advice, respond to what they believe to be a genuine romantic advance, buy puppies online, and, more generally, dodge scammers, shysters and online lowlife. This book on Crown and the gambling sector extends my coverage in the areas of governance, financial crime, risk management, and true crime. It is a career highlight and I am grateful for the opportunity to explore the history, problems and the impact of the casino business in Australia and overseas.

A book like this can only be written with the assistance and encouragement of a range of people to whom I owe an enormous amount of thanks. I thank Michael Wilkinson, the publisher, for taking this work on. Michael and I first worked together when he thought I could edit an accounting newsletter back in 1995 at a time when there was a restaurant called Vivaldi's in The Great Space in Collins Street, Melbourne. That was a watershed moment. It has led to a productive, rewarding and challenging career. *Crown: Playing in the Shadows* began with Michael bouncing the idea off me and he probably figured my mind would go off on my equivalent of hyperspeed. Thanks also to Jess Lomas who has had to endure my quirks as an author in this process of getting the book together from cover art to proof edits and all of the other things that come with getting a book out the door. Her guidance on covers has always been welcome. The author might be the subject matter expert but that does not equate to being a marketing genius!

Colleagues in journalism that have been both encouraging and helpful along this journey. My eternal thanks to Peter Gleeson, the Queensland Editor for Sky News, David Speers, the host of Insiders the ABC, Ross Greenwood, the Business Editor at Sky News, ABC business journalist Dan Ziffer and former ABC anchor Quentin Dempster have been encouraging along the way. Each has offered guidance and support across the journey across three books. Each of these individuals has taken some time out of their busy schedules to provide feedback.

Every book any author writes is a journey, but the journey into this poke and prod into the casino culture did not begin with Crown Casino and the various issues that saw the casino business helmed by James Packer get a bit more attention from politicians, regulators, and heads of inquiries, I had been fascinated for many years by the way in which illicit networks such as transnational organised crime gangs sought to embed themselves in legitimate society. Gambling businesses in Australia and overseas attracted crooks and shysters in the same way as an outdoor barbecue attracts blowflies in the middle of a hot Australian summer. Newspapers, true crime books, and, much later, texts on criminology and social psychology as well as endless documentaries on free to air television and streaming services fed this interest which remains insatiable. There is a great debt I owe my parents for continually encouraging me to read and better myself intellectually given the fact that I was born with a rare disorder called hypoparathyroidism that meant that I was less likely to be a person that would engage in the kind of physical labour as part of a career. Their care, concern and encouragement over my 50 years on this earth is not taken for granted. My brother, Robert, walked the journey with his older brother when our parents were both taking me to appointments and hospital visits. Rob, Sally and the two nephews, Mason and Archer, have also walked the journey of this book in a different way. An uncle has been a little absent while writing this book. There is some lost time that needs to be made up before the next big literary adventure.

I took the time back in 2018 to seek out my personal medical records from the Royal Children's Hospital in Melbourne using freedom of information laws in order to better understand the way in which I was diagnosed with hypoparathyroidism all those years ago. It would be remiss of me to not thank the paediatric nephrologists, the late Dr David McCredie and Dr Harley Powell, who were critical in my treatment over those 19 years. I was a conundrum from day one and they managed to somehow help me and members of my immediate family grapple with something that few people understand because not many folks have it. I also want to thank the McCredie family for thinking of me and inviting me along with my family to attend the memorial held in Melbourne on 26 March 2022 for David McCredie. He passed away during the peak of the coronavirus pandemic late in 2020 and a memorial could not be held at that time. It was a privilege to be there and to remember the life of somebody who impacted on and saved many lives with his knowledge and his care. I am here because of that medical intervention—saying 'thank you' never seems quite enough.

ABOUT THE AUTHOR

Tom Ravlic is an investigative journalist, author and academic with more than 25 years' experience in reporting on and analysing politics and regulatory affairs for local and international media. He cut his teeth with almost a decade of journalism writing about accounting and finance and breaking stories for a range of print and online publications including metropolitan newspapers, business magazines, professional journals and overseas newsletters. Tom got his start with the industry newsletter *Chartac Accountancy News* and he has never taken a backward step.

Publications such as *The Age*, *CFO Magazine*, the newsletters from the Lafferty Publications stable on accounting, the Company Director and many others in print and online have benefitted from his depth of research and knowledge of a field often seen by some commentators as arcane. Tom is most proud of his investigative work that resulted in multiple cover stories in *CFO Magazine* while he was a contributor to that magazine between January 1999 through to December 2004. He returned to journalism in September 2016 after 12 years in professional associations in various roles dealing predominantly with regulatory analysis, government relations and risk management. His work has been published in *The Accountant*, the *International Accounting Bulletin*, *Crikey*, *PC and Tech Authority*, *The Saturday Paper*, *Acuity*, *Company Director*, and *The Mandarin* since his return to print.

His expertise in corporate governance, accounting and audit has been recognised with two casual academic engagements teaching auditing and assurance at both Deakin University and the University of Melbourne. A collection of his writings was published in 2005 by John Wiley and Sons in a book called *Readings in Financial Reporting* for the academic market. Tom has been a guest speaker at conferences, chaired panels comprised of regulatory figures from Australia and overseas and helped produce events designed to bring accountants and other professionals up to date with developments in corporate and financial regulation. He is a Fellow of the Institute of Public Accountants and FINSIA.

Tom spent much of the coronavirus pandemic in isolation completing further tertiary studies. He holds four university qualifications with his most recent being a Masters in Fraud and Financial Crime and a Masters in Terrorism and Security Studies from Charles Sturt University. These two recent qualifications and his coverage of business and financial matters created a unique mix of subject matter expertise that led him to write *Vulture City* on the Hayne Royal Commission, which was released in October 2019. *Rorts and Rip-Offs* followed in November 2020.